Northern Waters

A Trawlerman's Tale

by Ron Telford

Enjoy the Storm

R S Tel

First published in paperback by
Michael Terence Publishing in 2023
www.mtp.agency

ISBN 9781800945555

Michael Terence
Publishing

Acknowledgements

I would like to express my sincere thanks to the following people for their help and support in producing this book:

TOM SMITH

JOHN SMITH

BILL BUCKLEY

PETE WOODS

PETE NEVES

FRANK POOK

DAVID ORNSBY [of the Grimsby Heritage]

STEVE FARROW

PETER GREENE

DENNIS AVERY

FRED POWLES

DAVID POWLES

CHERYL TELFORD [Wife]

I also have to mention the enthusiasm and encouragement I have received from numerous people who have read my 'blog'.

Thank you for your support.

Contents

Introduction

The tales I am documenting are all from memory as during my period at sea I did not have time to keep diaries. My memories come flooding back whilst I am working as a tour guide at the Heritage Centre Grimsby and I apologies if my dates are not accurate.

I am just trying to talk about my life at sea and what it had been like on a trawler, working up to 18 hours a day with 6 hours sleep. Plenty of local people, on both sides of the river Humber sailed but never returned. I'm one of those lucky ones that did and that is why I am trying to relate my time at sea, I left school aged 15 years and 6 months. I had applied to go in the Royal Marines but could not join until I was aged 16. My father found me work at Grimsby Dock Offices. My father worked at the Tax Office and I think he wanted me to follow in his footsteps. My duties involved taking mail around the fish docks as a Junior Clerk.

I saw the ships moving about in the dock and I was fascinated how they looked. I asked one of the fishermen, 'How do I get a start on the trawlers?' He pointed me to the Fisherman's Exchange where I enquired about going to sea. I was given a form for my parents to fill in but when I got outside, I filled it in myself.

At this time my father had started courting again. I had sadly lost my mother when I was only 10 years old. For me there would be no one to take her place. My father moved in with HER and I was politely told to 'piss off'. I've not always been an ANGEL but hey that's growing up. Anyway, I moved in with my grandmother and her sister which happened to be in the same street were my dad was living. After one trip, to sea we had our own flat.

I can clearly remember the summer of 1965.

My father remarried and I went to live with my grandmother at her sister's house. Whilst I was there, I met my cousin, Trevor Baskombe, who was then the Mate of the Gillingham and he asked if I would like to do a pleasure trip to sea. I nearly bit his hand off at being invited. He told me what I would need to wear and that we would be away for up to 21 days. He gave me an old kitbag which was carried over your shoulder. When filled I walked with a swagger in the garden.

The day came when we sailed. It had been a hot summers day and my cousin picked me up in his taxi. I arrived down dock and was given a bunk to sleep in, with a locker for my clothes etc. My grandmother gave me a cake tin filled with jam tarts, date slices etc. as a treat. When we sailed, I went on the bridge and watched as the crew went about their business, working as a team. We duly arrived at Iceland and I was amazed by the scenery, more so at night, when on clear nights the skies began to dance with the Northern Lights. I learnt how to clean fish and when the weather had been a little rough, I went down the fish room. The time passed quickly and it was soon time to go home. This is when fishing had me hooked. I was never seasick and I think going on the Waltzer's helped me to keep my balance which does help when the ship starts tossing and turning in heavy weather.

1

Boston Weelsby

Going to sea for the very first time, do you feel apprehensive, of course which is only natural. Welcome to a life changing opportunity. You go aboard a fishing vessel where you are met with different smells to your nostrils. Some are good (not many) and you soon get accustomed to them. The smell of fish on the decks hits you first and then over a 3-foot step you are passing the cod liver oil boiling area. Walking down an alleyway you see the galley which smells of coal smoke. There are two areas with places to eat your food and I soon found my place! Just ahead is a door leading to the Engine Room which clearly states 'KEEP CLOSED AT ALL TIMES'. There was a smelt of diesel and various odours which I could not identify.

Behind me was a deckie who asked me who I was. I told the man my name and he took me down some ladders where there were a number of rooms (cabins). These did not smell very nice and had a distinct smell of human sweat, staleness air and damp. At the end of the alley was a larger cabin in which four bunks were located. I had been designated a top bunk on the port side which had a tin tray bent over the wooden side. I soon discovered that this was an ash tray. I placed my over- the-shoulder oilskin kitbag which only had twine around it to keep my clothes together.

One of the old deckies said that if I rolled him a few everyday he would then make me a lanyard for my bag. I said; 'It's a deal!' When the time for a ciggie came I did my part and before we had reached the fishing grounds my kitbag had been done. It took the old dickie just under the hour to complete. I found myself rolling his cigarettes for the full voyage. Now I wonder who had the best deal but you live and you learn. Going up the ladders a lad, about my age, followed me up. I soon found out that he was the galley boy. We both went ashore to the ships outfitters to get a few bits to take to sea. I had my bedding with my wet gear which I took to the ship. With the help of a couple of younger men, I took it to my berth and introduced myself. I think one deckie had been called Roy and the other Pete. In later years we remained good friends. When making my bed up and putting my gear away, I had forgotten about the smells but it soon returned. I kept thinking; 'Will I ever get used to this!'

I heard some loud sounds, like an air compressor and then some tapping noises. This was the sound of the engines being fired up for sailing. The sound of a loud voice screaming; 'STANDBY! WE ARE LETTING GO SOON!' filled the air. I had already changed into some working gear, carefully putting all my gear away. I was told to follow the two young deckies who said; 'Come with us and keep out of the way!'

After coming out of the focsle we are now walking to some ladders which will take us up to the main alleyway. When suddenly a giant of a man shouted; 'Who the effing hell are you?' I looked at him and told him; 'I'm the deckie learner.' He replied; 'Do as your told. You're here to learn!' With the next breath he was saying; 'Hurry up on the deck!' Moving quickly, we approached the Whaleback. The order was shouted from the Bridge; 'Let go forward. Let go aft!'

The ladder from the quayside to the ship was pulled up on to the whaleback. Three men and myself carried it aft and tied it up to the portside handrail. I now had a new task which was helping to put away the stern ropes and then securing the ship ready for sea.

The weather was fine with a calm sea and looking over the ships rail I noticing how quickly we were travelling and how small the DOCK TOWER became as we left the land. Coming past two big forts which were named Bull and Haile which had been manned during the 2nd World War. We are now just able to see Cleethorpes Pier, with little dots which were actually people enjoying the morning sunshine. We had soon left the sight of the beach. On the port side was a large red lightship with the word SPURN written on its side, with a large rotating light. This helped mariners to navigate the River Humber. As we passed the ship started to lean to port, as the course had been altered with a Northerley heading.

I was just about to light a cigarette when I heard THAT VOICE which I now knew was the Mates. As he came nearer to me, he bellowed these words; 'YOU! YOU! NEVER GO ON THE DECK BY YOURSELF.

ALWAYS LET THE CREW KNOW WHERE YOU ARE GOING! I'm not allowed on the deck by MYSELF. That's how we lose men!' Later in life I knew that he had been right. I made sure I adopted the Mates WORDS.

The time was now approaching dinner time. I washed my hands and found the MESSDECK which was quite large with a banqueting style table. The galley boy came in with platters of food which I seem to remember enjoyed. In the afternoon I was called to the bridge to hand in my Registration Paper and on returning to shore I would be getting a Port Record Book which was like a Passport for Fishermen. I wondered whether I will take to life at sea.

Prior to joining the ship, the Grimsby Exchange told me what I would need for sea - warm clothing etc. plus waterproofs, gloves and boots. On the day of sailing, late November 1966, I was supposed to sail in the Boston Wellvale but I was moved to the Boston Weelsby, as the other deckie learner knew one of the crew. Both ships sailed together to Iceland but during the voyage one of the Wellvales crew members became ill and they were taking him in to Isa fjord for treatment when they ran aground. The crew were taken off by breeches buoy. This was the 12 December 1966 and thankfully, no one was lost or injured in the incident but it made the local papers. Unfortunately, no one had bothered to inform my relatives that I had changed ships and they believed I was on the Wellvale when she ran aground. We went in a few days later and we took the Wellvales crews personal gear home. The Icelanders re-floated her a few months later and I think they renamed her 'Ran'.

It seems strange, as growing up in the 50 and 60 I spent most of my childhood days playing in Weelsby Woods. I think at this time Wally Nutton was Skipper of the Weelsby and took a shine to me and eventually made me up to a full deckhand. We had an elderly crew, 'Odd job Goddard' was the winchman, Bill Patterson deckhand and Bill Smith deckhand, all of whom had been third hand in their younger days.

When we got up in the morning there was a strong smell of embrocation oil (horse liniment). They gave me lots of praise as a deckie learner. I had to speak to the Mate and Thirdhand for a daily job lists which gave me a lot of confidence. They then made me 'foreman dayman'. The job lists consisted of making spare wing bellies and baiting etc. I didn't quite know what they were but it had been a method of making me learn different parts of the net. I didn't, earned a lot of money but learnt a great deal from these 'old timers. I was in her till about 1968 and then she went to South Africa to finish fishing.

On a certain ship, I will not name, I had been called to the bridge by the Bosun. I duly arrived on the bridge after walking through the engine room and up to the wheel house. I had been told to take a mug of tea or coffee with me. When I arrived on the bridge most of my drink had been spilt either going up the ladders or down the walkways. I hadn't found my sea-legs at that time and every roll or sudden movement would make me stumble here and there.

I was told to put my drink into a pot rack and take over steering on the ships wheel. In front of me was a rudder indicator which was half red and half green for port and starboard. Above my head there was what looked like a periscope, with a mirror and light which was the compass. The course I had been given to steer was NORTH. I had been told that the BIG DIAMOND had been North and to keep it on the ships heading. After a couple of what seemed like minutes, the heading started to change going towards the West. I put the wheel a little to port and the course changed quickly, the wrong way. Now the wheel was turned to starboard and quickly again went past North towards the East. The bosun just kept laughing at me saying that I was 'chasing the compass instead of steering the ship'. With time I would have the steering under control. I was taken off the wheel and given a compass rose which would help me to learn the skill of being a helmsman.

The Bosun sent me below just before 2100 hours. I had tried a couple more times steering the ship but only for short periods of time. I took my empty mug down with me and gave it a wash in the galley. I noticed a large platter of meats with various lumps of cheese which the cook had prepared for supper. With a lump of cheese in my hand I walked down the ladders into the after focsle. A few lads were having a little party in the cook's berth so I decided to turn in to get a good night's sleep. This was practically a waste of time as the sounds grew louder as time went by. I put the pillow over my head trying to reduce the sounds. I eventually nodded off but it must have been well past midnight. I heard the Bosuns voice so I knew that the bridge watch had changed.

At 0700 hours I was called out for breakfast so that I could work with the daymen. I felt as rough as hell without even having a drink! The daymen looked as though they had not had any drink but the staleness of breath gave them away. The galley boy has not turned to having been seasick most of the night. The bosun asked if I would help the cook out until lunch time with the weather being a bit fresh. With the weather freshening I took his advice, wishing that I had not.

0800 hours I had all the pots, pans, plates, including the knives and forks to wash. I had to scrape porridge and beans from some of the pans. I soon learned to soak them first which made things easier. The ship started to roll a bit and my next task was to peel a full bucket of spuds. Whilst I had been doing this the cook had been making bread. This was my first insight of watching the dough being made. My next chore was to prepare carrots, the cook said that he would do the cabbage etc.

Just before 0900 hour I was told to make a kettle of tea for the morning brew which consisted of using an empty bean tin and half filling it with it with large tea leaves. This was topped with sugar, poured into a large silver teapot with boiling water poured in to nearly three quarters full, followed by with half a tin of evaporated milk stirred in to the mixture. When this was finished, I was told to shout to the lads on deck 'TEA O!' I was not needed in the galley until after 1100 hours so I made the most of my time chilling out. I poured a few drinks of tea for the daymen. The engineers came up from the engine room taking their drinks with them.

I popped to see the galley boy but not for long. He had the same colouring as the HULK, bright GREEN and bye did he stink of sweat and sick. As I left his company, I told him that he must eat something, otherwise he would just be sicking bile up and this would hurt his stomach.

I was going toward the accommodation ladders and the mate had been making his way up. When he reached the top, I climbed up myself. I-saw the mate step over the accommodation step and onto the main deck. I thought that I would pop my head out for a bit of fresh air after seeing the Galley boy but then I noticed what looked like the mate having a wee on the deck. I walked back towards the galley and hearing the sound of water along with a few cuss words and out the corner of my eye I saw the mate coming in off the deck, wet through! He looked at me and I **had** to say it; 'Is that why you must let people know that you're going on the DECK?' **Sorry but I'm not repeating His Reply**

At lunchtime I gave the cook a hand to carry the food in to both the officer's mess and the crews mess. The food had been placed in large bowl like platters of sliced meat and Yorkshire puddings. The next platter had a three-way divider containing mashed potato, carrots and swede together with a large jug of thick onion gravy. I nearly spilt the gravy on the Mate as he gave me such a horrible look which made me think that he was going to have a go at me. In the officer's mess were the Skipper, the Radio Operator and 'knobhead' [the Mate).

I couldn't help overhearing the Skipper making a remark that the ships were catching lots of fish at the North Cape which meant absolutely nothing to me. Twenty minutes later I went back into both messes to collect the meal platters etc. I was then back into the galley to wash all the dishes. I then had to refill the platters of food ready for the second sitting of crew members. When I had taken the last bit of food into the crew's messdeck I was told to get mine. This was when I met Taffy Fisher who was a greaser on this ship. Sometime years later I met his son Tommy and we became great friends for life. Sadly, he passed away leaving a void in my life but what memories.

Just before 1300 hours both messdecks had been cleared of food. This is when the cook surprised me by telling me that when I had done the pots and pans, he needed me to do another bucket of spuds, cutting them into chips. Talk about taking the piss. I was just settling down to do the dishes when the Bosun [Terry Waters] came into the galley and told me that he would wash the pots with me having to dry them. The plates were put into the racks, knives and forks back into the messes, pans and platters laid over the oven which soon dried them for storing in their places. Terry did the potatoes and completed then by making chips.

I was told to grab an hour which I did. The next thing I remember was being called out for a bond issue. I waited my turn and soon proceeded to the bridge and in to the skipper's cabin it looked like a small shop. Tins of Quality Street, Kiora orange juice, Old Friend, Old Holborn, Golden Virginia, [hand rolling tobacco), various cartons of cigarettes, Marlborough, Kensitas, Capstan Full Strength, matches, soap Typhoo tea and tins of evaporated milk. I didn't realise how much bond had been available. The skipper lent me a pillow case to carry my bond to my berth. I was just about to turn away when I heard him say; 'You've forgotten this!' and he quickly poured me a Colman's mustard jar full of rum. I gently necked it back and took me three goes but I kept it down me. I must have looked funny to the Skipper as he kept laughing at me as I walked away.

I went towards the galley and noticed that a deckhand had been helping the cook. He came over to me saying that you have helped the cook this morning and he left you to clear the mess up but he won't get away with it with me.

It was soon my turn to have my tea (2nd sitting) and I sat down putting food onto my plate. The Galley boy came in looking very pale and gaunt. He gently put a small amount of food into a soup bowl and he slowly managed to eat something. After having my fill of food which was gammon, eggs, pineapple, chips followed by a strawberry duff sprinkled with designated coconut and topped with a thick custard I peered my head into the galley to say thank you to the cook. His reply was; 'NO, THANKYOU FOR THIS MORNING!' I went aft to the bathroom, washed my hands, brushed m teeth etc. Slowly I retreated towards my berth where, on top of my bunk were some magazines. My first introduction to Gardening!

With the weather being scruffy, the daymen didn't call me out but 'he who must be obeyed' (the Mate) summoned me to the bridge. I was told to relieve the helmsman taking a turn at the ships wheel. The course was set to North half West. I held on this heading for maybe a couple of minutes, with the similar outcome as previously of chasing the compass. I was told to come off the wheel after twenty minutes or so. My next task was to look out the bridge windows for any shipping movements etc. I was asked by the mate if I had seen anything untoward. I turned around to tell him that all seems well. In a nasty voice he barked at me saying that I had been told not to turn around and to keep a lookout! I muttered under my breath that he should have done this whilst having a piss on the deck.

Just before 1500 hours the Mate went on the deck leaving me with his two watchmates. They told me not to take it to heart and he was just showing off his authority.

The wind had started to freshen with a small spray of water just coming over the whaleback. I had just been given the ships wheel when the ship dipped her head with the Mate on the foredeck. Suddenly, we scooped a sea which came over the whaleback drenching the, Mate. He came flying onto the Bridge and looked at the Compass heading and noticed that I had been on course. He went to his cabin to get a change of gear. On his return he said that I could 'piss off now!'

Going aft I had another little chuckle at the Mates gear hanging over the Engine Room hand rails dripping wet. After the evening meal I sat in the messdeck watching the crew playing cards. The Galley Boy appeared looking almost normal with a cigarette in his hand telling everyone that he didn't realise how bad seasickness could be. I turned in soon after but not before having a quick glance at the gardening magazines.

It only seemed like five minutes when I heard a voice calling my name and others for breakfast. Just after 0800 hours I was putting on my wet gear for the very first time. Firstly, I put on my thigh boots with an extra pair of socks. I then donned my bright yellow waterproof frock but to get it on correctly your head had to be put through first and followed by your arms which were threaded into the sleeves, followed your head through a hole and then pulling it over your shoulders. We had to wear a muffler (fisherman's scarf) which helped to stop any water going through the hole where you put your head. The first time that I put mine on I felt like a Penguin. I found it very awkward to walk in until I had worn a few times. I was not on the deck very long as the weather was beginning to freshen. This time tomorrow we should reach the fishing grounds. Time to get the gardening magazines out until I am needed.

The trawl had been in the water for nearly three hours. I was told to go to the winch at hauling time which I did. Standing in place, the warps were released in the towing block. Behind the winch there were two wheels used for guiding the trawl warps and keeping them level. It looked easy but with me, being about ten stone wet through, I found it quite difficult turning the wheel under pressure. With a little help from the bosun, my first task had been completed. I was then told to go aft, near the after-trawl door, to watch how things operated. The trawl doors soon came up, both making a loud noise and a chain was passed between two brackets which were secured by large hook.

After the dhan lenos came up, on one arm a link with a rope had been clipped up which led to the winch barrel. When it had been heaved on, just below the ships rail, this part was secured by a clip with the rope made fast to a cleat. All hands then started pulling in unison on the net. Soon, with quite a bit of effort, the trawl had tapered enough, allowing ropes and beckets to be attached which would soon pull the cod ends alongside the rail. Using a large becket which was put into a lifting hook enabled us to lift the cod ends on board.

I was informed that this haul was about 40 baskets of fish. Not too bad for a first haul, I was told. Soon the cod ends were over the side again, followed by the rest of the net. Two slips which held the bobbins in place had been released. The bobbins were attached to the quarter rope which had been held on by the cleats. The order was given to release, making sure that nobody was near any bights of the rope. Ropes were then released quickly followed once more with the shooting away of the gear. I was told to grab a brew and a smoke as we will soon be cleaning the fish in the pounds.

The time came to clean the fish and I had been sent forward in the pounds alongside the fish washer. I looked at how a couple of the lads were gutting the fish. They seemed to open the fish at the gills, place four fingers inside, then cut the fish across the nape. Then, all in one swift movement, the knife went all the way down, opening up the fish's stomach. A quick cut above the livers etc. released the fish's stomach. The removed livers were placed in a cane type basket, either for boiling or pouring into a holding tank. It took me several goes of doing the cleaning with different types of fish. I was told that if I found a 'tusk' (rubber like fish) I was to give it to the bosun. I learnt very quickly and I only did this once as I soon found out that it was a wind up. Once or twice, I had to climb into the fish washer to release the fish. On completing the gutting, I had to jump in again to clear all the fish out. I'm glad that I've got the first haul out of the way. I must admit to being aware of the dangers on the deck and having to be mindful of the surrounding and be extremely careful. Fishing was one of the most dangerous industries in the world.

Being at sea I must confess my first trip seemed like an adventure. Being up for eighteen hours a day really takes it out of you. Hauling the nets, shooting the nets, putting them back in the water were all extremely physical activities. The weather made the ship feel like a roller coaster. The water coming over the ships rail sometimes made me feel scared but the more that it happened seemed to make me have more confidence. On a couple of days, the weather was borderline fishing. This meant that I wasn't allowed on the deck. I thought to myself I can catch up on my sleep but at sea it doesn't work like that way. Although I was not allowed on deck during trawling operations, I would be sent down the fish room chopping and shovelling ice. Doing this for a couple of days meant that every bone in my body ached. I was so pleased when the weather changed and I could get back on the deck, especially as the mate had been in the fish room with us. He had me shovelling ice, throwing fish, then packing it in to the storage areas. Putting boards over the fish followed by a layer of ice and constantly putting fish away. Different species of fish had to be separated but 'he who must be obeyed' just stood near the sorting table smoking. I said; 'Are you just standing there or are you giving us a hand?' That was a wrong move from me as he came over and backhanded me across my face. I can still feel the pain today, just as though he had just hit me. Judgement day for him would come two or three years later!

Coming out of the fish room as the weather was improving, I was soon back in the fish pounds. The bosun noticed that I had a swollen lip with a blood shot eye. 'How have you done the damage to your face?' I told him that I had slipped in the fish room. He told me to be careful in future. A few days earlier it had been bitterly col. We had a broken trawl which had to be repaired. One of the deckies took over filling the mending needles. When the Mate grabbed me to hold up the net whilst he used the needle. My hand slipped as the ship rolled and with that the mate hit me with the needle on top of my knuckles which had been painful, as my hands were so cold. The bosun called me over to him and gave the mate a rollicking telling him; 'There was no need for that!' I never went near the mate again.

After a few days without incident and the weather being fine, we were fishing at Cape Bank, Iceland with fantastic views of large mountains covered in snow. We were just about to shoot the trawl when the Skipper shouted from the Bridge; 'You can Stow the Messenger this time!' I didn't know what it meant but suddenly the crew became instantly happy. I asked what was happening and they told me that stowing the messenger meant that we were going home.

Finally, our fishing operations have stopped and we are going home. We had 1,700 kits of fish but we still had plenty of things to do before we docked in Grimsby. Repairing nets, putting away all the deck boards, washer and gratings. All the internal cleaning had to be done and everyone did their share. The Skipper asked me to clean his cabin saying if I did, he would pay for my bond. I was pleased to do this as it got me out of polishing all the brass work.

We arrived in dock and tied up at the fish docks. We were the second ship in line with not too much fish to land. We should make a good trip. Stepping off the ship after three weeks at sea with my kitbag over my shoulder, I seemed to be staggering down the pontoon rolling from side to side. After a few moments NORMALITY returned. I arrive at my Nan's house who had been living at her sisters. I placed my kitbag down and my adrenalin was sky high as I spoke about my voyage. Nana had made 'Cowpie' especially for me and I remember how nice that the pastry had tasted. I then noticed that a small cup had been place under the pastry which stopped it from becoming soggy. After my tea, one of my uncles came to pick me and my nana up. I had to bring my kitbag with me and I asked where we were going but I was told that it was a surprise. We soon arrived at our destination. Whilst I had been at sea my Nana had got us a flat to live in. Going inside it had been basic furniture and beds but it was a place we could call home.

The very next day just after 1100 hours I took a bus ride down dock. Outside our Office men had gathered waiting for the pay office to open. I was told to go on the pontoon and I was directed Arthur Lacey's for my fry of fish. On reaching my destination I asked for my fry of fish but I was told that I did not have any as the Mate had taken both mine and the Galley Boy's. Going back to our crew someone asked 'Where's your fry?' I told him what had happened. He went to the see Johnny and soon returned with two parcels of fish, one for me and the galley boy.

One by one the crew took their place at the cashier's window. My turn duly arrived and I picked up nearly £20. I felt like a Millionaire. The Skipper went inside the cashier's office, not before telling me to wait for him. On his return he gave me £10 telling me that he knew what had happened on his ship. He said that I didn't complain but he wanted me to know that he had cleared him out of the ship. I didn't understand what he meant until one of the lads explained that the Skipper had sacked him.

With money in my pocket, I was given a lift down Freeman Street in a taxi stopping at Burton the Tailors. I went inside with a crew member, as he was being seen to, another man came up to me and asked if he could help. 'Yes please!' came my reply; 'Can you make me a suit?' 'What colour?' he asked; 'Navy blue' my reply. 'How many pleats?' 'Four please!' Then, in a flash, a tape measure came out to take my measurements. I felt like royalty. At this point in my life, I almost always had hand me downs. Now, here I am having a suit made to measure. I also purchased a pair of shoes and was gifted a white shirt, a blue tie and a couple of pairs of white socks. Now I have the Fisherman's Uniform. I was feeling so grown up and having only done one trip to Sea. From the tailors we met up with a few crew members in the Ship Hotel. I was asked if I was old enough to drink by a barmaid but the lads said; 'If he's old enough to go to sea then he's old enough to drink!' I think I only had about four large bottles of Hewitt s finest ale and I was put into a taxi with my fry of fish. I had a couple of hours sleep when my grandmother woke me up. As I went into the dining room there stood a burly man in uniform. He introduced himself then asking whether I still wanted to be a ROYAL MARINE. My response was; 'No, I'm sorry. I want to be a FISHERMAN!'

After Landing Day, I had decided to treat my nana from my landing money. I also let her have my wages that I had sent home just keeping one pay packet for myself. This will enable her to buy foodstuffs and to help with the rent, gas and electricity. She worked as a QC at Eskimo Foods, working long hours, including shift work. After my first trip at sea, I now feel like an adult. Maybe it's because from being a school boy, I am now working with grown-ups and at sea, in such a short space of time, I feel more confident in myself.

After having a cooked breakfast, I was given a key to the flat. I feel content because I have a roof over my head and money in my pocket. My elder brother at this time had been in the Merchant Navy and with it being the weekend I decided to see my brother and sister. I walked to my dad's house, knocked on the door and my stepmother answered. She said; 'Ooh it's you! What do you want?' My reply was that I wanted to see 'MY FAMILY!' She made it clear that she was not happy to see me and she replied that there was no one in and promptly SHUT THE DOOR IN MY FACE!

Although I was upset by her treatment, I decided there was no point trying to speak to her and I moved along and decided to do a little shopping. I went into Rumbelows and put a small deposit down on a television. When I told my nana what I had done it made her cry. We only had a small radio for amusement, furniture had been gifted or second hand. I didn't mind as I had my own bed AND a wardrobe. This was my little sanctuary.

I must admit, my nana really spoilt me. She knew that the life I had chosen would be hard as with her husband and brothers had been fisherman. She understood my work and in a short while it was time to go back to sea. My only regret at this time, was that I started to lose all my childhood friends as I was working away at sea. However, I soon made different friends who I worked with. Now, it is over fifty years ago when I first started fishing but I still see and chat to fellow fisherman.

I also found that I became stronger quite quickly, more confident and with just a couple of trips as deckie learner the Skipper promoted me to deckie trimmer, then on to a full deckhand.

Random Memories

I remember being a young deckie on landing day. Some pubs didn't like the 'deckies' going in certain bars or rooms, as they were for reserved for Skippers and Mates. Talk about class distinction. Hodges was one such place. So was The Angel snug at the back and The White Knight was another. Strangely, however, we were allowed in at night time. The Mariners was another such pub and so was the Oberon. After the cod wars anyone was welcome.

I loved going in the Red Lion, especially 'the ladies of the night room' with local girls. For some reason I always felt safe in there knowing that no harm would come to me. If we made a bad trip, someone would make sure you had drink. If you made a good trip, they never expected a drink in return. I remember the barmaid named Mary and I'm sure it was Bonzo's mum. She would send me home in a taxi if I had too much to drink. The 'girls' made sure that the young deckies came to no harm.

There were plenty of good pubs about. There was Cairn's, The Wellington Arms, Cottee's, White Bear all great pub and most with entertainment. I didn't like Darley's ales very much but it had a fantastic atmosphere. There was singalong in one room and a quiet lounge. I didn't care for the Lincoln Arms or the Prince of Wales. I always thought that one of the best pints was from the CLEE PARK with Landlord Jock and his wife Mary. Just to make things CLEAR these memories are a long time before I met my wife – just in case I get in to trouble!!

I can remember in 1967, just getting my deckies start in the Boston Weelsby. I had been going as trimmer, wireman and fish room man but now that I was able to splice wire and mend the nets having been taught by Sid Croft. This man had time and patience with me and I believe I was taught by one of the best. My first trip deckie I was made up to foreman dayman where I had to report to the Mate and Bosun each morning, going to and from the fishing grounds. I was given a piece of paper listing things that needed to be done or repaired etc. I came to learn all about belly baiting's, squares and wings and was shown how to finish on a quarter mesh. I must admit, half the orders at first were new to me but I soon adapted to them. After a couple of trips, I was put on the Mates watch thinking that I would have a boring time but no, not at all. He taught me basic chartwork, such as, how to make a bearing of any two given points of land and lastly how to use the Decca Navigation Equipment. I can also remember two trips later I had been put in charge of the deckies watch with Bill Smith and Alf Goddard who both built up my confidence.

A couple of years later I can remember being away at Christmas time on the Norwegian Coast. We had an Indian Summer, gutting in smocks and thigh boots, with very little mending and a decent catch. We all returned home with a decent suntan. The very next trip it blew nearly every single day but we still managed to earn a decent trip out of it.

Young and carefree at just 21 years of age! I wouldn't say having the time of my life but I was doing a job that I enjoyed and working with men who would remain my friends for LIFE! The only person to understand a fisherman, is another fisherman and of course, later, their WIFE.

Recollecting the early years of coming in from sea with a kitbag slung over my shoulder, rolling to and frow on the pavement, as I had not become accustomed of being back on dry land. Feeling confident and sure of myself. After making a good trip and going to Burton's [the Tailor] to be measure up for a new suit which for me was generally navy blue with a six pleated jacket and 21" trouser bottoms complete with a new shirt and tie. Part of the ritual was also to have a haircut at Billy Raymond's which was sometimes on tick. We only had a short time to enjoy our hard-earned money. We had docking day, landing day, a day in dock and then the next day back to sea. Trawlermen were a special breed of men. I am proud to have been one.

I fondly remember my younger days whilst going into certain pubs where the soles of my shoes would stick to the carpet. A coal fire would be burning in the corner giving a welcoming atmosphere. Music being played on the piano with the ceilings thick brown with smoke. Lonely deckies leaning up against the bar chatting up the barmaids or sometimes the barman [without naming names].

The laughter and the banter, with deckie learners telling everyone how good they were at mending and splicing. Telling everyone who would listen how useless the mate and bosun were. Two pints and they were legless mainly due to sleep deprivation. The Licencing Laws which seem strange now [Opening at 1100 hours and closing at 1500 hours then opening again in the evening at 1800 hours and closing at 22.30 hours]. During these closed periods it was off to the Exchange or the Alex Club until 1700 hours. It was then home for a quick wash and change then off down to Cleethorpes for the night.

On a Wednesday it was 'Grab a Granny Night' at the Winter Gardens. Other nights were spent at the Kakadu, The Flamingo, Bunnies Nightclub or The Sands which had a good landlord and landlady being Tom and Joan Lee, who brought many famous turns to the area. Of course, not forgetting Taddy's on the sea front. It was crap Ale be it had a brilliant atmosphere with Alva Cromer playing the Guitar or the piano and the Dolphin Disco had been the place to have fun. HAPPY DAYS!

2

Princess Elizabeth

In.1968 I joined the Princess Elizabeth with Albert Brown as Skipper. We were going to Iceland and on the second day out, just before lunchtime, I was awakened by loud noises. As I opened the cabin door two Geordies came into the berth quickly followed by the Skipper. All I heard was 'bang, bang, bang'. Then the door flew open with the Skipper saying. 'I won't have anyone chucking their hands in with me.' The two lads came out the cabin and continued working. They were as good as gold all trip. The Skipper – Judge, Jury and Executioner!

I can remember an incident February 1968 which scarred me for life. I was on the Princess Elizabeth with Albert Brown. The weather at the time was atrocious with a full gale and severe icing. All hands had been called out. We were at Rittur Hook dodging the weather. We were under the shelter of the land, chopping ice from aloft. The wind factor was ice-cold and all hands had been called to the deck to chop ice. ALL WATCH BELOWS WERE STOPPED. Was I scared - the answer is YES! We were heading into Isa fjord for shelter. All the weight aloft on the mast and rigging had built-up with of ice. With a hot drink down us and wrapped up as best we could we ventured on the deck using knocking out hammers, fish room axes, together with crocodile spanners.

We all began knocking the ice away and with the wind screaming through the ships rigging things seemed quite eerie. Hitting the metal on the foremast, the ice soon became loose, with big lumps falling all around us. My task was to clear the windlass and control area so as to drop the anchor when things became safer which was when the top ice had been removed. After a couple of hours, we all went off deck to warm up and get some hot liquids down us. After a while we all returned to the deck for another go. All the ice that we chopped down had to be thrown over the ships side. Slowly but surely, we were making headway onto the foredeck. We worked as a team, clearing around the trawl gallows and otter boards. I was feeling quite exhausted as I had been up 18 hours previously. The skipper sent a dram of rum around to boost morale and to keep us going.

Breakfast time soon came around and we all went aft for something to eat. Halfway through the meal there was one hell of a noise above the messdeck. We quickly scrambled on the deck to discover half of the mizzen mast had snapped off with all the radio wires being loose and flying about above our heads. The wires were eventually pulled tight so as not to go around the Radar Scanners.

The Skipper asked to go alongside to get vital repairs done which was granted. Going alongside there were more ships tied abreast to each other getting shelter. This experience made me realise what a dangerous profession I had chosen as a career. We were lucky but other ships were less fortunate and never returned home! This incident happened at the same time that three ships from HULL were lost with all hands. When the weather abated, we steamed south. It is a time that I will never forget and rightly so, as so many lives were lost.

Random Memories

Another trip on the Princess Elizabeth I had been ordered early morning. I left the Kakadu (a Nightclub) at 0200 hours and I was supposed to be sailing at 0400 hours. The taxi took me down dock and I got straight on the ship. The taxi driver let go of the ropes and chucked them off the ship. I argued with him that it was not his job to let go of the ship and it should be the runners that did this. I was annoyed and so I jumped off the ship at the lock gates. I then walked home.

The next day I was summoned to appear in court. Before going to Court, I went to my doctor and told him I didn't feel very well on sailing day and he gave me a sick note. I appeared at the Magistrate's Court and when my name was called, I entered the room and sitting before me was my G.P. who was also a Magistrate. He fined me ten pounds with five pounds cost for failing to sail. As I left the courtroom the ships runner was waiting for me. He paid the fine and took me down dock. I then went out on the tug and re-joined the Elizabeth.

3

Prince Philip

I sailed a few trips in the Prince Philip with Ray Harries, Skipper Pete Almond, Mate, Stan Johnson, Bosun and always remember that we had a good all-round crew. We earned plenty of money but being single I mainly pissed my money up the wall, as they say!

I remember one trip when I was about seventeen. We had been iced up, with the weather moderating the Skipper decided to shoot the net. The trawl doors had been inboard. I was told to climbed up the forward gantry to pass the heaving wire (Gilson) on to the forward door to heave it out. I suddenly lost my footing, slipping off the gantry and landing on my back. The fall had obviously hurt my back and I had to be carried aft into the galley area, lying on a stretcher.

The ship went into Isa fjord because of my injury and I was taken to the Hospital. When I arrived, I was given a full inspection of my back, neck [which was in a brace] and all other areas I could have damaged in the fall. I was stripped naked and a young, attractive Nurse approached me to assist in the examination. Embarrassingly for me, my 'manhood' began to rise but a portly Staff Nurse noticed what was happening and stepped forward, slapping my 'manhood' and declared; 'WE WILL HAVE NONE OF THAT IN HERE!' Needless to say, my 'manhood' made a hasty retreat.

Fortunately for me I had only heavily bruised my back and my 'manhood' suffered no permanent damage.

Three days later I flew from Isa fjord to Reykjavik and stayed there for two days due to heavy weather. Eventually I flew home landing in Glasgow. At that time there had been a lot of trouble regarding gangs with the Police and at that time it was not a very safe area. At Reykjavik airport I had a bottle of duty-free whiskey, for taking home. I also had my kitbag with my clothes etc.

In due course I caught the train to Edinburgh and onwards to Newcastle. On this train there had been lots of football supporters travelling south to watch their team play the next day. I had been invited to join a group of lads and later on my whiskey came out with a party in full swing. I caught the train just after 1600 hours and destination was Doncaster for an onwards journey to Grimsby.

Unfortunately, I didn't get off at Doncaster and instead I woke up in Peterborough at nearly midnight. I was standing on the platform when a rail employee asked me where my destination had been. I told him Grimsby but I was advised that there was not a train to Grimsby until 0500 hours which was the mail and paper train. He then showed me to the waiting room where a coal fire was glowing in the fireplace. I opened the door and to my amazement all I could see were plenty of white eyes. I quickly left the surroundings, with the railman laughing at me. He then took me into the station master's room. He made us a nice cuppa with some food which he shared with me.

My advice would be; 'DO NOT GET DRUNK ON A TRAIN WHILST YOU ARE TRYING TO GET HOME!'

A few years later I had a disc removed in my back. The fall I had could have been the start of my back problem.

4

Broadwater

I joined the Broadwater in November 1969 with Raymond Evans as Skipper. I knew him through his brother at Beacon Hill School. It always seemed a pleasure going to sea in this ship with a great crew, plenty of fun and lots of laughter. Slim Hornsby was Mate but I can't recall who was the Bosun but maybe it was Roachy. We earned plenty of money and I always felt lucky in the ship which proved to be right for me.

I seem to remember that the Broadwater had been owned by a woman. I believe that you could enter the aft focsal by some ladders near the bathroom and by steps near the galley. On the bridge was a large steering wheel which was set back from the bridge windows and she was totally hand steering. We had a youngish crew, Colin Drevers, Freddy Almond (Pink Panther), Pete Bowman cook, Terry Knowles and a few more that I can't remember. I think that Eddie Grant joined the ship and left his taxi on the North wall.

We left Grimsby, maybe lunchtime. Watches and daymen set for duties. I was in George's watch. We sailed up the East Side of the UK and Scotland to fish the Southside of Iceland. We caught a quick trip but ran out of ice and had to run into land for more ice. I can remember this as if it was yesterday and as we were running into the land the Skipper said; 'Do, we fancy a beer?' My answer was of course; 'Yes'! He told me that it was on the bridge top, under the radar stack and I'm sure that the beer was Heineken. I took five or six cans down which we all drank, prior to lunchtime. After lunch we picked up more ice then soon sailed. We steamed a few miles somewhere near Hari Kari which is a fishing ground. Shot and hauled with a big bag of fish. We had a couple of tons of ice on the deck, as we were nearly full up but we now had to take the hatches off to put the fish in the hold. Job done and we were now bound for home.

The next day on watch we were asked once again whether we wanted a can of beer. Of course, the same reply was 'Yes please!' I went on top of the bridge and the beer had gone! We later found out that it had been the Pink Panther who struck again.

We steamed home and made a good trip.

Being single and care free I went out with a couple of the crew. I went into Arthur Burtons and was measured up for a suit which I would collect next trip. I went home to the flat where I lived with my grandmother. A few months later my brothers and sister moved in. On this occasion only my elder brother was living with us. Spent landing day and night down Freeman Street. The next day I met up with Terry Knowles and we went down Cleethorpes. The usual haunts, the backroom of the Dolly [Dolphin] with Elsie the barmaid who was a lovely lady. We then crossed the road to the Vic. [Victoria] Jack Portlock was the (gaffer) and then down to the Sub disco [Submarine] with Joan and Tommy Lee (gaffers).

We were down for sailing early morning and as it was a Sunday, I had been drinking all day with Terry Knowles. In the evening we met a few of my brother's friends and were having a really good night. That's when I glanced over towards the bar and noticed a girl sitting down behind the bar, messing about with her nails. When I looked at her, I knew that I could fall in love with her. I asked if I could have a round of drinks but she replied that she was not allowed to serve as she was only allowed to wash the glasses. Soon a barmaid came with drinks I had ordered and I asked the girl if she would like a drink. She had a coke and I believe during the evening I kept sending drinks over to her.

Sometime during the evening, I asked if I could take her out next trip. With a bit of persuading, she said OK. I asked if I could wait for her and get her a taxi home when she had finished her shift but she said; 'No thank you. I have my own car.' Laughing, I said; 'Good, you can give me a lift then!' She dropped me off where I lived and we made arrangements to see each other next time I was in dock. Three weeks later I went to the Submarine and Joan told me 'the girl' would be working that night [Sunday] and I should call in. I did not know it but Joan called to tell her I had been in asking after her.

When I first saw her, I was smashed as I had been drinking all day. To be honest I could not completely remember what she looked like and so I went in the bar for a drink before going to the lounge where 'the girl' was working. Joan had served me and afterwards she went to the other bar. A short while later 'the girl' came through to get some change and I recognised her immediately. We exchanged a nod and I waited until she finished her shift. Later she dropped me off and we arranged to meet the following evening as she was at work during the day. We got on really well and began seeing each other or 'courting' as they used to call it!

We have been married 51 years in March 2023.

I told you the Broadwater had been lucky for me!

Random Memories

Climbing up the Steep set of ladders and on to the Whaleback area, I heard a loud voice shouting from the bridge.

He was screaming at me. 'Can't you walk any faster? You're the last man on board. Put that bag down. Give them lads a hand coiling the bridles away and be sharp about it!'

My reply was; 'Get your effing head in and stick the ship up your arse!'

This took place as the ship was about to leave the lock pits. Suddenly the ships radio blasted out; 'Have you one of my crewmembers aboard you?' The question had been about me!

I had been in the ship stores when my ship had sailed. The ships runner had told me to go on one of our other ships and then transfer to the Brenda Fisher.

I heard this message clearly and the Brenda Fisher came alongside and as I was about to board, the Skipper who had given me a lift, shouted from the bridge wing;

'IF YOU EVER NEED A SHP, YOU CAN SAIL WITH ME!'

I will leave you decide how I reply!

5

Boston Kestrel

[Various dates between 1968 and 1972]

I can remember the Boston Kestrel coming to Grimsby in 1968. She had been laid up for a while and a Grimsby crew had to get her ready to sail again. All new warps had to be put on the winch, new lifting blocks, Gilson tackle, yo yo, all new weights bobbins, footropes, all had to be renewed, nets put on board and be made up. Sailing with mostly local lads and we all knuckled down as a team. The Skipper had been Bill McHasite from Hull. Whilst working alongside the fish room which had been full of maggots and sure enough, they later developed into flies (bluebottles). Eventually, everything had been cleaned and disinfected.

After about a week alongside we eventually sailed on the maiden voyage from Grimsby. We steamed to the North of Norway and called into Honninsvag. We were in for a few hours and I went ashore after breakfast and climbed a hill and then returned back to the boat.

During the morning five of the crew went ashore and found a van up the mountain near the cable car and decided to take it for a joy ride. The next thing they heard was a Police car following them. After a while, with the Police in pursuit, the van left the road and rolled down the mountain side and settled on a ledge. I seem to remember there were no major injuries.

The lads were locked up but were later released and we sailed again to the fishing grounds. On our return to Grimsby the five crewmen were taken off the ship.

The following trip, a new skipper, Derek Brown, took the ship away and during the trip I had been followed around the ship. The office had received a message from Norway that items had been taken from the van. I was unaware of this as I had not been involved in the incident but I think I was suspected of knowing something. Nothing was ever recovered.

Random Memory

I remember being asked to do a trip in the Boston Phantom with Skipper, Dave Sherrif and Mate, Harry Preston. She was the sister ship of the Boston Kestrel. At the time of the tragic loss of three Hull trawlers, due to a build-up of ice, Boston's decided to use the Phantom to test something new.

The ship was fitted with black inflation type bags which were used in conjunction when the ship iced up. The bags would inflate removing any build-up of ice. Another concept which had been considered was to put hydraulic clutches to be used with the winch mechanism. During the time that I had been in her we only had slight icing but when we used the bags they split. The bags needed to be constantly repaired.

The ships that we sailed with went home making decent catches with good prices. We caught half their catch and made little money. I only did the one trip and signed off to go in the Belgaum.

6

Boston Kestrel – Iceland

In June 1974 after a week at home and having a new baby daughter, I found it soul wrenching having to leave my home and family to make living at sea. Leaving the wife, now with two young children to look after was hard. I think that if she had asked me to stay with her, I would have done but she knew that as I was a trawlerman. I had to go away.

Taxi Picked me up at 0800 hours then taken down dock. I really could have done with extra time at home and feeling guilty leaving my wife at home with two small children, but my wife, being a skipper's daughter. (Bill Ferrand) understood that my work took me away from home. My father-in-law didn't want his daughter marrying me [or any fisherman] as he knew what the life was like. His wife having to be 'mother and father' to the children whilst he was earning a living. However, in later years we became close.

When we arrived on the dock, I took my gear to my cabin. I went into Vincent's to get my gear and bed issue. The evil one behind the counter with his dark rimmed glasses (Eric) asked me if I needed anything but with the history in what he tried to do to me pay twice I told him to piss off. I later went to Coleridge's especially for my gardening magazines. I went back on board with my gear and stores, I unpacked my things putting them away in lockers. I had just about finished when I was summoned to the bridge. Once up there the Skipper shook my hand. He has just returned to sea after suffering from throat cancer and his voice was now a whisper. I admired and respected this quiet man who had a great deal of skill and knowledge.

On the other side of the bridge was the compass adjuster and I could have done without this steering this way and that till the compass had been set which took about 40minutes. He passed the compass variation card then left to go on the Brenda Fisher then back to dock. Finally, we were on our way up the river sailing towards the fishing grounds. The mate relieved me on the wheel. Tommy Smith, who was also from Aberdeen, now living in Cleethorpes, seemed very pleasant. I went down below decks and saw the chief, Holy Joe (Jenkins) and the cook Pete Bowman sloshed and talking about Dolly his partner. Nearly every trip he was chucked out of the house then back the next day as if nothing had happened. But what a cook he was! I went down below to the party berth, had a couple of cans and drams, then bid my farewell and rolled in. I had 6 hours before I went back on watch.

Went off watch at 2300 hours slept like a log. Woke up a couple of times listening to the sing song that the lads were having in the focsle most of the crew did the same taking a bottle and a case to sea which I either brought the day before sailing or got it on tick the day we sailed. It is now a lovely evening as we are steaming down the east coast going north. In the distance the sky is lit up from the oil rigs in the distance and we could see the wake of our ship being lit up by phosphorus in the sea. I had a few yarns with my watchmates and what they did this leave (can't publish) and I did similar antics when I was single. 0300 hours soon approached and I was relieved by the watch.

I went to the mess and had a quick sarnie before I turned in. I woke up about lunchtime, to be told we were heading towards Aberdeen with a small job on one of our generators. We tied up on the supply boat quay and alongside a newish pub called the Quarter Deck. We tied up at 1700 hours and the Skipper took the bridge watch as he had arranged to see his brother. After tea a few of us went ashore to have a couple of beers in the Quarter Deck which was quite plush and by 2100 hours went back to the ship and sailed at 2200 hours. I went on watch again at 0300 hour until breakfast and worked on the deck until mid-morning when the bond was issued. I received mine which was a tot of rum with 12 cans of beer to take to my cabin. We had a lovely lunch of roast beef, Yorkshire puddings, roast tatties with the usual vegetables followed by some treacle duff. I went to my cabin for my afternoon siesta.

Went on watch at teatime approaching Duncansby Head. The skipper came out of his cabin and told me to make a course to Dennis Head. We were going through the Pentland Firth but have received a north westerly gale force warning and to get the daymen to check that everything is secure and battened down. I did as I was told and I went with them. After a few mutterings we proceeded on the deck. By this time, we were leaving the lee of the land and the wind was now screaming through the riggings. We all kept together putting extra lashings and chains were needed. We made sure the wedges were hammered in and it didn't take much longer than twenty minutes. When we were back inside making sure all the dogs were closed on the watertight doors.

I took my gear off and thanked the lads, with the words coming back to me here anytime if needed which was bit different to twenty minutes ago when they told me fluff off. Back on the bridge and we were beginning to rock and roll a bit with sprays of water at first then building up to heavy seas sometimes filling the foredeck but soon clearing the scupper doors, which we open only in heavy weather. The skipper kept popping on the bridge as we started to dip and dive. The radio operator handed over the weather report to the skipper and he in turn told us that we will be sheltering under the lee near start point and when the wind starts veering to the SW, we will continue our journey. When we arrived at start point, we were not alone, half a dozen other ships had the same idea and just after breakfast we were heading towards the grounds. I sailed a few times with Wally Nutten and we fished in some horrible weather. Has he altered? WATCH THIS SPACE!

When my watch was relieved at 2300 hours both the galley boy and deckie learner had their heads in the toilets being sick both looking as pale as a ghost. I don't think that we will see them tomorrow. Popped into the messdeck and had a cheese banjo lathered in Branston which is still one of my favourite foods. Shall I take one to the young ones. No, I'm not that cruel!

Called out at 0700 hours for breakfast and watch. I had a couple of kippers, toast with a mug of tea. The skipper popped his head in the galley and advised the cook to do a pan of shackles or sandwiches for lunchtime. He stated that the wind would be on the port quarter once we have left the lee of the land and to make sure everything was battened down. No sign of the galley boy but the daymen would give Pete the cook a hand. We are now leaving the lee of the land and we are nearly broadside to the weather. The seas were rolling up to the rail and occasionally one would come on board and fill the portside with water then quickly disappear back into the sea through the scuppers. The wind was now whistling through the riggings and making screaming sounds. Soon after we were able to set course to head to the east side of the Faroe Islands which will now put the wind on the port quarter making it a comfier ride so to speak.

As lunchtime approached the weather started to abate and we altered course again to go down the west side of the Islands. We were relieved at 1230 hours by the mate's watch. I made my way to the galley area and the cook had done a full roast dinner, ignoring the skipper's advice, as most cooks did. The galley boy had appeared with green gills, telling me that he thought that we were sinking with the sound of water he could hear on the main decks. I tried to comfort him, saying that it's not always as bad as we have had it and that we have better days ahead. I must admit my first trip I nearly shit myself, scared - who me. YES. I had my lunch and soon after fell asleep.

People don't realise that whilst standing on the bridge in heavy weather how much you ache, mostly your legs but the rest of the body too. Just after 1600 hours I was called out for my BOND. Waited my turn on the bridge I took my allocation which was a case of beer with a ration of rum. Teatime soon arrived but I was still full from lunch so I just had a few chips with an egg thrown in. After tea had a few games of rummy to pass the time away until watch time which soon came upon us. Relieved the watch as we are nearing the Faroe Islands, now the northern lights are giving us a front seat display once more. Herring gulls and fulmars are passing on both sides of us, nearly in touching distance, looking for scraps of food. We were listening to radio Luxembourg till about 0230 hours when we began to lose the station. Watch relieved us, passed on our position etc and bid my farewells. I went below, brushed my teeth, had a quick smoke then crashed for the night. I reckon it will be about lunchtime when we will be at the fishing grounds.

Just after lunch we shot the gear into the water. after mending a few rips where the net had caught up in the scupper doors and having checked all the shackle connections, we began to lower the net. Swung a turn in the ship then finally payed away the warps, after a few moments we used the messenger hook to pull both warps into the towing block and the order came, 'ALL SQUARE' which I shouted. We were now doing the first tow of the trip. The lads came off the deck and into the mess deck area and an issue of rum was given. We were now fishing in an area called 'the whaleback' and we began towing towards the land.

The first haul after 3 hours produced about 40 baskets which is about 25 ten stone kits off fish being an assortment of different species of fish but mainly squaddies and ling. We then put the net back over, without any issues and cleaned the fish. Then teatime was upon us. I relieved the skipper on the bridge and when he returned, I had mine my meal which was cowpie with fresh vegetables lathered in daddies' sauce which is another of my favourite foods. Just after tea we came fast. I heard the screech of the warps being pulled followed by the knocking out of the warps. I then fell asleep and was called at 0300 hours to shoot the net. We were now fishing on 'the kidney bank', with the Belgaum alongside us.

Fishing has not been too good today with five and ten basket hauls. We had seventy this morning but now the fish has taken off. Skipper told us to lift both trawl doors up and we steamed for a couple of hours or so. It's now lunchtime and we had halibut soup with fresh busters to eat. A t about1400hours we shot the net. The weather is calm with dense fog which chills you to the bone. After we had finished on the deck I popped onto the bridge and was politely told not needed as he was trying a new tow. Wally didn't speak much after having his throat operation and for deck signals, he used a whistle Which were 1 to heave, 2 to stop heaving, 3 to shoot the warps awa etc.

At 1700 hours we hauled the net with eighty baskets of mainly large haddocks(jumbos) with a sprinkling of cod and squaddies. It would be a good living if we could catch this every haul. Teatime was soon upon us. I then went on the bridge and told to just keep on a given course and to keep a good lookout on the radar. We were 15 miles east of the Horns, limit being 20 miles. Whilst looking after the watch I notice that there had been a can of coke in the pot rack so I decided to take a quick sip with my throat being dry. I discovered it was laced with whisky, ha-ha. The Skipper soon returned to the bridge and sent me down for mine, roast beef, shredded cabbage, roasters, carrots, mash with a plain duff with onion gravy and Manchester tart for afters. I said my thankyous to the cook and made my way to my cabin. I had a quick glance at my gardening magazines, looking at the roses and chuckled to myself. You get a few pricks on these!!!

Called out at midnight saying we have just hauled with 40 baskets of mainly haddocks again. Just about reached the fish pounds when told to lift the nets straight away. knocked out the warps and soon the trawl doors were hooked up, followed by the dhan lenos. The bobbing crashed on the deck, net pulled in and the order came, 'Drop the doors in!' This was done quickly and we were steaming southeast. The reason being for the speed was that a boat appeared on the radar coming towards us. It was The Tyr, an Icelandic gunboat. We were now being followed and we soon reached the 20-mile fishing limit. When the gun boat neared us and over the tannoid a voice shouted that they knew that we were fishing inside the limits. We have got away this time but they'll catch us next time but they never did. After the excitement we went back into the fish pounds to clear the fish away. After a couple of hours, the fish had been cleaned. We had a quick cuppa in the mess as when we hauled noticed a couple of holes in the belly head. Repairing this took about 30 minutes then back into the warmth. My watchmates and I popped onto the bridge for our evening nogging of rum. We were now going to the North Cape as fish had set in with a few good hauls reported. First bit of gash (extra sleep) and we didn't waste any time climbing into our bunks.

Over the last two or three days, according to reports the fishing is quite slack. We had a couple of hauls at Melrraka and averaged 40 baskets with a few holes in the belly head. We were just told to lace the net and get it back over the side. The weather has turned very cold at minus 6 although the seas are calm but this doesn't make it any easier. Tried at Grimsey Isle which has, been a waste of time. We are now at Horn Bank, towing towards Stromness and both Capes North and Little Cape. in the process of hauling, with slight icing, wearing layers of clothing to keep warm with mittens covering my hands.

The mate is on the winch whilst hauling with the last 50 of warp in. Told to hold the short mark, 25 fathoms. Ship took a turn out herself then the command to start heaving again. I'm in position at the after gantry standing by with the dog chain, when all of a sudden, the doors came up at full speed. The skipper pushed the emergency cut-out switch and stopped further operations in retrieving the trawl. I'm glad the after gang, me included, had quick reactions, as no one had been injured.

I had to laugh after the event as the mate took his hat off and started jumping on it lol. He did this on numerous occasions when things went wrong. Strange man. Winch motor was then reset. This meant that we could retrieve the trawl which we did without any issues. The net came onboard with 20 baskets of fish, with a couple more holes in the bellies. The Mate was called on the bridge, most likely for a reprimand in private. He later came down sheepishly saying sorry to us all.

We are now on Cape Bank and the nets been put over with the warps put into the towing block. Snow was beginning to fall. Went into the fish pounds and within 20 minutes we were taking our gear off ready for tea. I had a quick smoke then onto the bridge to relieve the skipper but was told to ask for a fish sarnie and a pot of tea to be taken on the bridge by the galley boy. I took my place in the officers' mess with no sign of the mate. I went to look for him. He was sat in his cabin and when he saw me, he apologised and said he could have killed us all aft. I just said come and get your tea, it was an accident. I've never told the wife but I guess that she knows now. I must admit it happened on a few occasions. Just a lack of concentration due to harrowing conditions with sleep depravity. Such were the conditions working as a trawlerman.

We have been fishing at the Cape Bank for three days and averaged 50 baskets each tow which is a decent living. No more incidents with the mate on the winch. The weather has now taken a turn for the worse with heavy snow in blizzard conditions and occasional hailstones. Standing behind the winch, shooting the gear away just after breakfast, with a head to wind. Shooting really takes it out of you, with the snow and hail hitting you face on whilst trying to read the warp marks. Eventually the job completed and now standing in the warmth trying to light a cigarette, which is no easy task, but we just get on with it. Back into the fish pounds gutting the fish. Soon this trip will be over then we start it all over again. We just get on with it as it is our way of LIFE.

We have only a couple of days left for this trip to end and it has been quite a pleasant trip. We had to change the fore door out which is no easy feat, having to take the fore warp over the whaleback, attach it to the spare door, use your Gilson wire to pass under the door, attach to the ships rail, then heave the door over the side, then slowly heave on the fore warp to bring the door up. These things never happen in good weather. Do we complain? Not, not really, although sometimes we MOAN!!

Over the last 48 hours we have caught nearly 500 kits of cod. The Skipper asked the Mate for a tally and was told 1600 kits but hoping to turn out 1700 kits. We have been fishing all by ourselves, and ended up fishing just of Isa fjord gully. Some really good-sized cod with a few haddocks and a few large plaice. A couple of baskets were put aside for taking home (shush) don't tell anyone). It's our little secret. The ship came fast just after breakfast. The net had been stuck firmly on a submersible object. We tried heaving then lowering the net but with no joy. On the third attempt, however, we became free.

The doors came up followed by the dhan lenos, with a few headline floats and the bobbins intact. We had lost the rest of the trawl. The order came to put the spare net on. This net had been lashed on the portside which we then heaved across onto the starboard side. It didn't help much as the weather began to freshen up. Parts of the trawl snagged up to the fish washer and gratings. In just over an hour and a half we had the net ready for putting over the side. I went on the bridge to let the skipper know and was told that we have a bad weather forecast with southerly winds and was told to drop the doors in. We are going HOME!

How quick things can change from day today. We are cold and wet and have salt water stinging our eyes but then the trawls are lashed down, gratings are put away along with the deck boards. The Cook had asked for a couple of baskets of fish for meals which always tasted better after being on the ice. Battened down the hatches, put all the dogs on the doors opened up the scupper doors, extra lashings put here and there to stop anything becoming loose. The morning dram was dished out by myself and was told we have one left for the river.

Lunch time approached and I had a bowl of Halibut soup and looking forward to cow pie for tea. The mate rolled out at lunchtime said he would take the first watch. 1300 hours and I heard the engines as they gathered speed to take us home safely.

After my lunch I turned in but not before reading my gardening magazines. A good gardener that I followed had been Millington's roses, with another called Debby likes orchids. After half an hour glimpsing through the reading material I soon fell asleep whilst thinking of HOME.

Just before tea I took a shower, put on a fresh set of clothes and a splash of aftershave [English Leather]. I made my way into the officer's mess met with a few strange looks. Cow pie had been the main meal for tea with vegetables and all the trimmings. There was also fish was if you fancied that instead. I had my fair share, went on the bridge to relieve the mate.

We are just passing Reykjanes's a headland just before you get to Reykjavik and it being the capital of Iceland. The northern lights are giving us a master show this evening. It's such a relief once more having a good catch of fish and it makes it more worthwhile having a good crew as well. We are beginning to lose the lee of the land, the ship is beginning to dip its head into the wind and seas, throwing water over the whaleback with spray reaching the bridge windows. With the occasional dollop falling on the main deck, we are now abeam of 'Snowy' which is a large volcanic mountain and I was informed that there is a large prison situated in this area. Our course is now set to pass the Faroe Islands sometime late tomorrow afternoon, then onwards to Dennis Head.

We came off watch just after 2300 hours, had a quick smoke with s cuppa then turned in for the night. We will be back on watch at breakfast. The weather has not got any worse and it's a force 6 gale. I turned my bunk light out listening to the sound of water rushing onto the decks, shortly I fell to sleep.

We have been steaming home for nearly 15 hours and I was in a deep slumber when the mate woke me up and said we will be shooting the trawl for a couple of hauls. I asked, 'Are you kidding me, for effing sake!' I've used different words. I soon found myself up and dressed. I was sitting in the MESSDECK when the crew came in sleepy eyed and full of it. They asked if I knew what was happening and my answer was 'NO'. Just lighting my second rollup when from out of the tannoid a voice came, saying we can go on the deck and unlash the trawl and the rest of the gear.

I picked up a new cod line then made my way forward to the deck. It had taken nearly 30 minutes to unleash everything and put the trawl doors in the standby position. I threaded the new cod line through the meshes and tied the knot. The order came to get a drink as we will be putting the net over in 15 minutes. The weather being crap we could do with the warmth inside the ship. We had a quick mouthful of warm tea; a smoke and we were back on the deck putting the trawl back over the side. Soon all square was called and we were now FISHING AGAIN! We put a few deck boards up in the fish pounds and returned to the warmth of our beds. I didn't wait up for breakfast feeling pissed off with oneself.

0930 hours we hauled the nets. Doors up, dan lenos just coming out of the water, when a sudden whoosh was heard as the cod ends appeared. We heaved the bobbins over the rail, followed by the headline floats then manually pulled the net at the rail. When the net began to close in, we used heaving beckets to pull the rest of the slack net up. The Skipper sung out the bridge window that he would be going astern and to take some fish out of the cod ends. We found the halving becket leg, put the Gilson into it and as this came to the rail the tackle hook had been put into the lifting ring to heave the cod ends aboard. We did this same procedure four times, then the last bag came on board which consisted of 250 baskets of extra-large coley. We were told to start gutting them which we did after a quick smoke and two hours later told to put the net back over and shoot away again, which we did. One hour later the decks were clear of fish.

Lunchtime soon came and went. The order came to lift the nets which had been in the water for two hours and when we retrieved it with just 50 baskets of cod which seemed strange. The last haul we caught coley and this haul cod. The order came, 'Drop the doors in, we're going home!' I'm sure that I've heard these words before. Smiles came back on the faces of the crew once more as well as LAUGHTER!

After the cod ends were emptied of fish on to the deck, we dropped both doors in, chains were put around the bobbins along with a few ropes lashing on the trawl. A quick smoke followed while we retrieved our gutting knifes and gloves. Some of the crew, like me, only used mittens to haul the net in. I climbed into the fish pounds, just settling down to gut the fish when I was called on the bridge. I made my way up, thinking the worse, as I reached the bridge door, the door opened and a bottle of rum was passed to me along with the dram glass. I went into the fish pounds with the bottle hid in the trawl and told the crew we were shooting the net again. I have nearly caused a mutiny but I retrieved the rum and told them I was fibbing. I was then called every name under the sun. We had plenty of banter on the deck as it passed away the hours gutting in the pounds. I passed the rum and glass down the fish room, with voices coming up that we have the best Skipper in the fleet!

The fish was swiftly put away and this time we cleared all the deck boards away along with the gratings. Finally, yes finally, we are going home to our loved ones. Teatime soon approached. I went on the bridge to relieve the Skipper. All hands were clear of the deck. The engines were put onto full speed. The weather had become Northerly and we now had fair winds to move us along with a little more comfort, instead of heavy rolling of the ship. The Skipper and Mate came on the bridge after their tea and I was relieved to get my meal which turned out to be a mixed grill with all that went with it, followed by apple crumble and thick custard. I soon devoured mine whilst in the crews messdeck. My next watch Would be 0300 hours. Should I have a shower? NO! I am going to wait until we are nearer home!

Who would imagine just over thirty-six hours ago we had just finished fishing? We had dropped the doors in and started steaming home. Having passed a few boats going to the grounds, the Skipper gave a few the information where we had been etc.?

Our course line home, we passed Dennis Head at a distance of three miles, then all the way to Rattary Head and Buchaness. We kept the same distance off and this is where you begin to smell the land. With large herring gulls sitting on the forward rails with a few just gliding idly pass the bridge windows. During nightfall we could see the beams of lights coming from various buoyage and lighthouses along the coast and occasionally cars in the distance.

The Crew has been kept busy prior to docking. We have overhauled the trawl, given the decks a good scrub with chloride of lime, as well as all the internal cleaning. Just after breakfast we passed Flamborough Head, then followed the 23d on the Decca Navigator which took us to Spurn Lightship which we passed 50 minutes ago.

As we were heading into the fish dock, on the quayside stood Bill Battie, alongside Joyce, the Skippers wife carrying Smokie their Yorkshire Terrier. We soon disembarked and all headed to our homes with a few going for a pint or two. Richard asked if I wanted a pint in the Humber. I declined the invite.

We landed next day with just over two thousand kits and made £26,500 for a 20-day voyage. I was asked in the office would I go back in the Concord. **My Reply...?**

7

Boston Kestrel – Norway Coast

Steaming through the fjords with lots of fantastic scenery, of not just the land, as the skies were well lit up with the Northern lights. The trawls were all prepared. Having to make two extra pairs of cod ends with extra cowhides. It's mid-January and I'm on the Boston Kestrel. It had been my second trip there as deckhand. The previous trip we had the episode with the lads in a van and I'm one of two deckies remaining from last trip. Eventually we drop the pilots off at Honninsvag and we are now heading to Cape Cherney and Canin on the Russian coast which will be almost another 24 hours to get there. The weather is not ideal as it is a Northerly 5 with Heavy snow squalls, with slight icing.

Eventually on the grounds and the nets have been in the water for less than two hours and the first haul contained 40 baskets of plaice. The next haul was the same. Then we changed trawls as there was little left of the net when we finally had it onboard. We were told to drop a danbuoy (marker system whilst at sea) which we can find and changed the trawl over. Now having to make up a new one which is not an easy task anytime but with the weather being so cold it is more difficult. We are using bare hands joining the trawl parts together. We changed the trawl five or six times and repaired the cod ends many times more. We averaged about 50 baskets of plaice at a time. As we shot the nets away again and made our way back into the fish pounds, the fish was frozen solid which made our task of gutting the fish much harder.

Eventually we were told to just throw the fish into the washer ungutted. At the end of the trip, we landed 1,400 kits and made a decent trip. I was asked if we were going back to the same grounds, would I stay in the ship. My answer was; 'Just give me the pen – TO SIGN OFF!'

Random Memories

Another trip I can remember in the early 70s, as deckhand on the Boston Kestrel, we had well and truly iced up. Orders were given to chop all the ice off her and we would be running into Isa fjord. This we duly did and by mid-afternoon there were about 6 ships tied up breast to breast. As we tied up a couple more tied up outside of us. Unbeknown to us the Skippers had arranged a get together on the Real Madrid (Cocker Mussel). After tea the Skipper, Derek Brown, sent down a couple of cases of beer which was about 4 cans each and issued a dram of rum to us all. He stated that if any of us caused any trouble he would sack us when we docked. The Mate, big Johnny R, put on his uniform which Boston's provided, to wear whilst in Harbour etc.

At about 1930 hours the Mate came in our cabin and he threatened us all as well. He then asked if we thought he looked smart. Brynner Newland said that his tie needed straightening, which Brynner did. With this off he went to join the get together. At about 2200 hours we heard an almighty bang and then our cabin door opened. There stood the mate, bleeding from his head and eyes, with no shirt or jacket, just his tie. One of the crew asked if he had, had a good time. He was told politely to eff off. The next day and until docking day nothing was said about the incident. One rule for one, so to speak but the mate never went in Cockers' company ever again!

Another trip I can remember in early 1972 when I was in the Boston Kestrel, fishing at Vestmanyer Islands in Iceland. We caught 1,700 kits of large cod during a trip which was 12 days dock to dock. We had very little mending and I think that it had been my 2nd trip since I had got married. I came home, staying at a friend of the family's bungalow.

We had a good night's sleep and I had been standing outside the building when I had been told all our fish had been condemned. Talk about being shocked. When I eventually got down dock, I found out that it was true. The fish had been condemned because it had been too oily after eating mackerel and herring. I WAS ABSOLUTELY GUTTED. The Trawler Companies were not too bothered. After all THEY OWNED ALL OF IT BETWEEN THEM

Whilst in the Kestrel an unforgettable trip which I recall very clearly happened when I was Bosun. We sailed about lunchtime and the lads had a few beers from the pubs prior to sailing. I had been on the bridge steering the ship in the river when the bridge door was flung open by the galley boy, saying that the crew were fighting and there was blood everywhere. The mate, who was getting on in years, was on the bridge and he told me that with the Skipper's approval to sort it out.

I went down into the after focal and heard a bit of shouting but no fighting. I discovered three of the crew had been having a few drinks. Two of them had rolled in to sleep it off but the third person tried to pinch a bottle of spirits from behind a sleeping crew members pillow. He caught him in the act and the thief was struck with the bottle over his head, near his jaw line. There was blood everywhere! I used direct pressure to stem the flow of blood and with the aid of the Chief Engineer we managed to stop the bleeding. The Skipper decided to take the ship back in dock where the Police took all the crew, myself included, to the Police Station for statements.

The wife had been informed that we were coming back in to port and followed the Police Vans to the Station. After a short period of time, we were allowed home and told that we would sail again the next day which we did without any problem.

Yet again, another trip on the Kestrel I recall a happier occasion which I clearly remember in 1972. I had been gutting the fish in the pounds when the skipper called me on the bridge. There he gave me a telegram which read:

'BABY BOY! BOTH DOING WELL!' I was then given a bottle of rum to share out with the deck crew.

Another incident that spring to mind was when we had just sailed and were doing compass adjustments just outside the harbour. A crew member, who didn't want to sail, decided to jump over the side. He was picked up by the Brenda Fisher, who was thankfully standing by to take the compass adjuster off when the adjustments had been complete.

A further incident occurred when we had just let go off the North Wall. A crew member went into the steering flat to cause damage so we couldn't sail. This person was locked in the steering flat. We tied back up on the quayside and the person involved was then arrested. He had a mental breakdown and was sanctioned never to sail again.

On a different occasion a crew member took an axe to the bridge trying to smash the controls. He eventually had to be restrained and put on a naval craft and taken into Newcastle for medical treatment, I believe.

8

Northern Queen
– North Cape, Norway

I obtained my third hands ticket in 1973, whilst working for
Boston Deep Sea Fisheries, Grimsby. I took my ticket to
the office and was told that they had no position available
as they only had 8 ships at the time. I walked around to
Northern Trawlers and the answer was the same.

I had only been home for a few hours and when I received
a message to return to Northern's as they have a third hands
position for me on the Northern Queen. I have never been

on an oil burner before which had a steam winch and I thought to myself; 'This is going to be a challenge'. I then discovered that my father in-law, Bill Ferrand was taking her away as Skipper. Am I worried? **YES, I AM**. I am just hoping that I know some of the crew which will make things a little easier for me. I later learned that the Northern Skippers didn't know me and I had no experienced as third hand, as yet. That had been the reason they would not take me. After this voyage, I soon proved that I could do the job.

I needed to go down dock to the Fisherman's Exchange to pick up my holiday pay. The wife took me in our car to save me getting a taxi. I had 184 days, which included college days and I received £24 [The equivalent in 2021 would be £257]. I also picked a chit up for bedding (horse hair blankets) 1 flock mattress and new waterproofs for the deck. I went around to Vincent's on the North wall and that horrible salesperson 'little Eddie or Ernie' [I can't remember his name] who charged me twice, for the same stores a few trips ago, £8 40p [robbing sods]. I eventually received my money back but it took a while.

I came out of the stores, found where the ship had been berthed, with the stem to the quay. I climbed the wobbly ladders up to the whaleback and threw my gear onto the foredeck which had taken two journeys up and down the ladders. Eventually I went aft to the great smell of the liver house not a pleasant smell but one you got used to. The watchman approached me and asked who I was and I told him. He took me to my cabin which had a smell of sweaty socks, a hint of oil with a touch of fish thrown in similar to the great smell of BRUT. Not going to complain, as the accommodation was adequate for my needs and I'm sure I would soon get used to the smells and creaks of my new challenge. Had a quick guided tour and thought; 'What have I let myself in for.' I didn't want to leave the wife on the quay for long. so I came down the ladder, entered the car and we went down Freeman Street for a few bits to take to sea with me, as we will be sailing in a few days.

On sailing day taxi came 2 hours prior to high water. The ships runners liked to get you down early. Happy Sizer or Snowy Parker came for you. I never ever treat them. Usually, I was picked up first then driven round the Nunny or Waltham areas picking up crew member and then back to town. This running around really pissed me off. Finally down dock to the ship berthed on the North Wall. I would through my bag on the whaleback and head for Coleridge's (outfitters) to get a few bits, gutting gloves etc. Then head back to the ship to meet the crew and put my gear away. Most of the crew knew I was the skipper's son-in-law, and thought I would be here for an easy trip. Little did they know what the skipper had instore for me. I went to my cabin and changed into my work gear. The time being 0100 hours and some of the crew still had alcohol in their system sitting on the locker and were quite sociable with me. I was quite pleased as I knew a few familiar faces. The mate came down and said I was needed on the bridge as we were preparing to sail. I then realised the difference between a deckie and thirdhand. This would be a new challenge.

I went up to the bridge via the engine room. The Skipper was waiting for me and I said my pleasantries. I was then told to stand behind the steering wheel and put 20 degrees of starboard wheel on, then we went astern, wheel midships. moving slowly, we proceeded to the lock gates. Within minutes we were heading towards the Burcom (channel buoy) and then heading up towards Spurn Point. The steaming watches were then set. I took the first watch until 0300 hours. The Skipper stayed up with me and made sure I had been putting the position down correctly from the Decca Navigator and that I felt confident to take a watch and to complete the necessary paperwork. At 0730 hours I went down below with my watch keepers and had a quick bite to eat [corned beef sandwich]. I rolled in for a few hours of well-earned sleep.

On a clear evening steaming towards Savino (Norway) with the loom of the land in the distance and the companionship of a few sturdy herring gulls gliding passed the ships sides. Over the stern phosphorus is being lit up from our propellor and leaving a trail of sparkling water behind us. One of the watch keepers went aft to bring a pot of special to the bridge (tea brought from the bond, usually Typhoo, or Brooke Bond PG Tips]. It was good at times just being with your watch mates and talking about what you did on leave. Most fishermen became friends for life because not only did we look after each other at sea but we also spent many a time having a few beers in the local taverns when we were home. Looking up into the sky which had an abundance of shooting stars cascading down from our solar system and entering the earth's atmosphere. Both watch mates, [Gerry Proudlove and a kid from Brigg] were looking with me at natures finest. The Northern Lights were flickering through the sky, in the distance. People pay thousands of pounds to see this but we just take it for granted.

I had been called out at 1000 hours as the Skipper wanted to see me. I went onto the bridge and was asked if I had used a Walkers Tailing Log before and I said that I had. This consisted of chord rope, a spinning wheel and a fishtail which when screwed into a log clock was then gently laid over the stern which, when operating, would give the speed over a period of time. On diesel vessels the speed counter was built in to its systems. At the end of each watch the readings were taken and recorded into the log book.

Lunchtime soon arrived. I went into the cabin (Officers Mess) and had my meal. I felt very strange eating with the officers and I felt really uncomfortable as I had always eaten with the lads in the messdeck. The cook, (Clubfoot Bert) and the galley boy brought the food in on large serving platters with ample food.

After lunch I went on the bridge to take over the watch but the Skipper said that I could go on the deck with the daymen and whilst they were working, I had to end for end the CODENDS, by myself. This meant stripping everything off, including chains, lifting straps, halving beckets, cowhides and chopping all the cod line meshes off. This was no easy task, using a hacksaw and sharp knife. Let the challenge commence.

This task took me until teatime to get about half the work done. I would finish the task the following day. Just before teatime the Skipper gave out the bond and said we would be going into Lodigen (LOFOTEN ISLANDS) around breakfast time tomorrow. This was to pick up the pilots as we were going to drop them off at Honninsvag and would start fishing at the North Cape as the boats already there were getting a steady living.

Sunday 0800 hour, just after breakfast which consisted of bacon, egg, mushrooms, sausages, fried bread and fresh bread and butter. We approached Lodigen Pilot Station and on the mountain side there was the Coastguard and Mountain Rescue Team who gave us permission to enter the area of the Pilot Station. The pilot boat approached us and two pilots came on board. Old Snowy and K B S who were regulars on our ship. The first thing they asked was; 'Is it fish for breakfast.' and the answer was 'NO,'

The Pilot Cutter then passed us some carton milk, venison and a box full of French torpedo rolls. Both Pilots were taken to the bridge whilst I went to finish the cod ends. Everything finished by mid-morning with new meshes and a new cod line. Had a couple of goes tying and releasing the knot when the Skipper sang out, 'I hope that you are tying it correctly.' My curt reply was 'Of course.'

After tea break, I helped to put the fish washer up with the day men. The weather outside had been quite fresh so we waited till now. All the pound boards with gratings and jockey boards were put in place. I honestly didn't realise what the difference between a deckie and a bosun (thirdhand) had been, until now. Chartwork came easy, navigation was a pleasure to do, being in charge of the deck crew so became second nature but eating in the officer's mess was not easy of me as I felt like a fish out of water. Mind you, today I went in the crew's mess, with some banter between the lads and myself.

I had an hour before lunch to try to familiarise myself with the steam winch. A diesel/electric winch stopped almost immediately when you put it into the stop position and I soon learned that on a steam winch you had to take a few turns off the operating wheel to slow it down. I'm sure I will master it but for the first couple of times I will watch the mate and winchman. My confidence is now beginning to strengthen.

I went on watch at 0300 hours with heavy snow and blowing a gale. Pleased that we are not in the open waters KBS [Pilot] is on my watch and he is doing everyone's head in – 'north a quarter east,' 'north, a half east,' 'north a quarter east,' and I'm sure that he is doing it to wind us all up. Daylight is soon approaching and the weather has dropped away under the lee of land again. Just approaching Tromso and I took the wheel. Same again 'half this way and half that', 'head for the light in the middle', soon passed it.

A fresh smell of bread came onto the bridge and we knew that the cook had been upset with the fresh rolls that came from ashore yesterday. My watchmate went below to call the watches and daymen for breakfast. Skipper came up to the bridge and told me that a pair of bridles (cables) which were 60 fathoms, from last voyage, need to be chopped down to make into 40 fathoms and I had to do them after brekkie. When breakfast had finished, [I had mine in the mess deck again, my little protest)

I went on the deck to splice the wires, chopping the right amount of wire off and allowing for the splices. I was helped by the daymen. The eye was secured and spun to take the turns out to open the wire. It took nearly three hours. Sore hands, aching limbs and we haven't put the net in the water yet. 'Roll on home time.' I muttered under my breath.

KBS was the nickname we gave to one of the pilots who guided you through the Fjords. We called him KBS because his favourite instruction was 'keep the barsteward straight'.

'm pissed off now as someone's grassed me up to the skipper saying that I have been eating in the crew's mess. I have had a right telling off and he finished it off by saying; 'You're not a deckie anymore!' Stayed up until lunchtime which was onion doff with a beef stew. Cooks' meals are ok and for tea it will be desperate dan pie without the horns, (meat from lunchtime) with strawberry sponge and desiccated coconut. Sleeping well on here. I had better go before the skipper catches me up.

Went on the bridge at 2300 to relieve the mate. He told me that the skipper had been impressed with me and said that I wasn't afraid of working. However, knowing my father-in-law (skipper) I could not imagine that he would tell someone what he thought. He would have told me 'Face to Face' whether good or bad comments. I'm sure he {the mate] grassed me up about mealtimes.

On watch with the other pilot (Snowy). What a difference and pleasure to be on watch with this chap. THE NORTHERN LIGHTS WERE IN FULL FLOW what a magical moment again. Came off watch at 0300 hours and we should be at Honninsvag about tea time. Had a piece of toast and cleaned the galley and messdecks in preparation for the cook getting up soon. Off I go now for a well-deserved watch below.

Up before lunch, had a quick shower and a change of clothes. There will not be many chances to have a shower once the trawl goes over the side. Weather is fine, with a nip in the air. Dinner arrived in the Officers Mess with Radio Operator, Skipper, and myself. We all tucked into the food when KBS (Pilot) and the Chief Engineer came in together to have their meal. Did I feel out of place, you may ask and 'YES' would be the answer. I quickly had my food and then had a pot of tea prior to going on the bridge. I relieved the mate at 1230 hours.

The Skipper came on the bridge and told me to go with him to his cabin. He told me again that my place had to be in the Officers Mess and to socialise a bit more and that he would do my watch as he wanted the greasing done and the top blocks [heavy lifting gear]. I am just so pleased that the weather is fine as I had to climb the mast, with just a grease gun and a few rags in my pockets. No safety harnesses. It had been pretty easy climbing up the rigging. The lads down on deck swung the Gilson block and then the tackle towards me to make life easier. Yo Yo block we just released it from its securing ropes and the quest had been completed. Took the chance of having a bit more practice with the steam winch, as well as tying the cod line. At 1430 hours the pilot boat came to take of the pilots off as we were nearing Honninsvag. On the pilot boat appeared KAARE who was the Agent for the fishing fleet. He had his hand into everything, dentist, outfitters, groceries, oil, fishing gear, etc. He passed up a large box of storm lighters to us which were sent to the bridge to be divided between the crew. Cleared the land at 1600 hours. Just started to release the trawl when the Skipper called out that we were going back in with a problem down the engine room. A message from the bridge said the engine job would keep us in overnight and that I had to stop aboard. GUTTED!!!!

Left Honninsvag just after breakfast feeling refreshed after a goodnights sleep. Some of the crew went ashore. They found a disco just selling soft drinks. They soon came back to the ship.

Later all the trawl had been unlashed and both trawl doors made ready. 1000 hours we put the cod ends on the yo yo (out hauler) then heaved them over the ships rail, followed by the bobbins and headline, with cans or bogs depending where you lived. The dan lenos were then lowered into the water. These are attached to the weight of the trawl and flotation. The ship then turned slowly starboard, then more wire was lowered which were called bridles which in turn were attached to a G link on the doors. With the pennant attached to the Kelly's eye, the slack wire was then attached to the door frame using a strip of cowhide and a small shackle. The order was given to lower the trawl door down to a given position [which was named short mark). The ships speed was then increase. The order was given to lower the warps (pay away). When the amount of warp had been let out the ship then eased in the engines and a special hook, called a messenger, was attached to the forward wire that pulled both wires into a towing block on the starboard quarter. This was locked in by a pin which a knot was tied onto to it stop it coming apart. It was then all contained by a block and chain [towing block]. The engine speed of the ship was then increased to a towing speed. The shout then went up to the Bridge to inform the Skipper that we were; **'ALL SQUARE AFT!'**.

The weather is like a milk pond not a breath of wind. We are fishing in the North Cape of Norway which is situated between the Norwegian Sea and the Barents Sea. This is in the area were the German battle ship 'Scharnhorst' was sunk when it came into contact with HMS Duke of York, on 26 December 1943. Only 36 men were rescued out of a crew of 1,968.

All around us there are plumes of smoke from several vessels fishing in the area. The trawl had been in the water for three hours and the crew stood by to haul in the gear. From the bridge the order came to knock out, release the wires in the towing block. The big steel wires came in at a steady pace. All crew members stood in their place. My first time at the winch, at the control, with two men using the guiding on gear (to keep the wires level on the winch barrels). The last mark prior to the trawl doors appeared and the skipper said he was taking a turn out of her by pulling the trawl in a tight circle. We commenced pulling the warps in. I started taking the turns off the winch control to slow the speed down.

The after door appeared first, it came up level. The chain was put through the brackets. The crew asked for slack wire to disengage the G link. The fore door then came up and the same happened, disengaging the warp and bringing the cables in. Up came the dan lenos and they were made secured at both ends. The winch was then taken out of gear and the winchman took over the controls so we could use the machinery to lift the trawl in. The bobbins (weights) came in first, quickly followed by the floats on the headline. The nets were then pulled in manually, as the wide part of net began to be pulled in, my worst NIGHTMARE, BECAME REALITY.

Pulling the first haul in with a decent catch of fish, we could see that the cod line had started to undo. As the weather had been flat of calm, we threw a grappling hook at the cod ends. We were then able to slack the net away a little and whilst the cod ends were alongside the ship, we put the Gilson hook into one of the bottom rope eyes of the cod ends. Using the long hawk, (long pole with a hook at the end) near the cod line, to guide it in. We then heaved the cod ends on to the deck and re did the knot. We then carried on with the pulling and heaving the net and finally the fish came aboard. The skipper said that I was one lucky fellow. Some of the ships that afternoon had the cod line adrift because the state of the tides. When it came to tying the cod line the next time, I used to open one side of the bottom of the cod line rope and thread one end through so that it wouldn't come loose. My self-confidence was growing stronger. We shot the net away again without any incident. I was then called onto the bridge and the Skipper said well-done. He then gave me a bottle of rum to take around to the crew. Finally, I think the skippers beginning to have faith in me. Teatime soon approached. I relieved the skipper for his tea and he told me that we were in for a nasty gale and that three ships had their cod lines come adrift. I then went down for my tea and began my watch below.

I was called out at midnight and was told 'That it's blowing a hooley' and we had come fast (the fishing gear stuck on the seabed). I put on my jumper and then my boots and went up into the messdeck for a quick drink and a smoke, just to wake myself up. Me and my watch then put our protective gear on and proceeded onto the deck. As soon as we went on deck, we began dodging waves that kept coming over the ships rail, as well as high winds. We had heavy snow swirling about.

The net had come free of the obstruction and the forward top wing had been ripped out. The rest of the net was on board including the cod ends with 50 baskets of large cod. I went forward to help take out the remains of the top wing when the mate appeared from the fore hold carrying a new piece of net with a couple of the lads. The net was passed to me and I laid it out and said that it was a lower wing. The Mate then shouted at the top of his voice, 'Can't you tell the difference between a top and lower wing.' The Skipper called us both on to the bridge and asked, 'What's going on?' The Mate gave his version saying that it had been me who brought the net up but the skipper stuck up for me. He told me to leave the bridge. By this time a new top wing had been put in place but needed to be attached to the rest of the net which took about 20 minutes.

I shouted up that we had finished and was told to lift the doors for 20 minutes. The doors were lifted and we went inside for a cuppa and a smoke. After 20 minutes we went back on the deck. Still heavy snow and we shot the net away head to wind. We had difficulty seeing the marks on the warp, not just because of the snow but the heavy spray of water coming over the whaleback. Soon the trawling operation had been completed and the shout 'ALL SQUARE!' was heard. My watch and I went on the bridge for our evening dram of rum. The Mate apologised in front of me and my watch and I accepted his apology but never trusted the man again. I left the bridge and went into the fish pounds listening to Patsy Clyne, Dolly Parton, as well as other country singers. Spray, snow and music - Oh the joys of being a fisherman.

Hauled at 0400 hours. 60 baskets of large cod. No ships in sight and winds have eased but bitterly cold. Dug out an old pair of woollen mittens which are warmer than gloves when working the trawl. On the horizon we were approaching what looked like a fog bank but 'those that know' recognise that it is 'black ice' which freezes on contact with metals and ropes etc. As we approached it, we could see the ropes etc. and steam from the crew's breath.

Mid-morning it had cleared away but is it a taste of the weather that we are about to see more often. We hauled the net just after breakfast, a bowl of porridge and a nice fish sarnie with a strong mug of tea which I enjoyed. The Mate came off the bridge but I just went passed him and straight onto the deck. When we hauled the nets there was very little fish but a heavy smell of decaying bone. A whalebone had wedged itself into the cod ends. We took it out of the net and threw it over the side but the smell lingered for well over a week, despite our scrubbing the decks and putting black disinfectant down. I still remembering the smell, as fellow fisherman will know.

Went aft after we had shot the nets and called onto the bridge to see the Skipper. Nothing had been mentioned about the incident with the Mate the night before. I was told to make a dan buoy ready which is large pole with cork floatation, a small anchor with a coil of rope and radar reflector. This had already been made up and tied to the portside rigging. We were fishing in 50 fathoms of water so needed at least 400 feet of line. This was made ready. At about 1030 hours we hauled the nets which had 200 baskets of cod.

We are still fishing on the Cape Bank but with the snow and now ice, building up the Decca navigator, in heavy squalls. is not reliable. We were told to standby. This time when we hauled to deploy the dan buoy. We hauled the nets, with 100 baskets of cod and a mixture of haddocks. We were then told to deploy the Dhan Buoy. It was then lowered over the side with a line and float to recover. We then lowered the anchor and line, into the sea and the Buoy held fast. We then shot the nets away and finished cleaning the fish.

I was called on to the bridge as one of the mast lights had gone out. I slowly climbed up the mast, with a few heavy rolls, clinging on for dear life. When she steadied down, I commenced climbing and reached the all-round white light. I undid the screw at the top and replaced the bulb. My watchmates shouted to the bridge but the light still didn't work. I then tried another bulb but same reply 'not working' came from the bridge.

I climbed down the mast with legs like Shaking Stevens. Those that know 'your legs feel like jelly'. I then went on the bridge and the Skipper said he would try the fuse bulb and when he changed it, hey presto, the light came on. Why didn't he try this first before sending me up the mast!! On most ships the skipper would give you a dram for going up aloft but not me.

We shot the net away before lunch and an issue of rum was dished out. I took the rum back on to the bridge and it was lunchtime. A pan of shackles had been the order of the day with fresh busters. The galley boy was still feeling seasick and we were nearly a week away. The Radio Operator typed the news that he received and posted them in both messes. The young deckie learner worked from 0600 to 1800 hours and seemed keen to want to learn about the job. In later years he became skipper.

Dinner time approached, pork chops, mash, peas and carrots. I went on the bridge after lunch and was given a bit more practice towing the net etc. It was nice to be on your own with no other ships in sight and having a steady living, I'm still sneaking in the messdeck but anybody reading this 'please don't grass me up' – lol. The mate keeps having a dig at me but I'm not biting. Well not yet, watch this space.

The mate called me to his cabin and he told me to close the door behind me. He then told me that I shouldn't be here as thirdhand because the Skipper was my father-in-law. To me that was NOT the case at SEA. I was being treated the same as the rest of the crew, if not harsher. I must admit that he gave me my start as third hand for which I have always respected him. Anyway, there was a heavy smell of alcohol coming from the Mate and I felt that it was my turn to speak. As I started to give him my opinion, he lunged at me. People who know me from work and ashore, know that I am not a violent man but I have always been able to handle myself. I pushed him back and then he stumbled to attack me again, then 'WALLOP' I let him have a backhander. He said that he didn't want me to hit him anymore which was fine with me as I didn't want to in the first place. I then opened the door and vacated the area. What to do now? Do I let the skipper know what has just happened? The answer is NO not until we are at home. We still have a job to do and have to get on with it. To this day what I did still hurts and none of the crew were told. PS even the wife doesn't know about this, but I guess she does NOW! Even now I still I don't like bully boy tactics.

Had a lie in (extra sleep). Called out to shoot the trawl at 0230 hours. Been steaming from 2100 hours. The dhan buoy had been put back into place on the port mast. The weather conditions were not very nice. Went on the bridge for our evening dram. The mate pointed to where it was and I had mine with my watchmates. I then left the bridge and not a word was spoken. Breakfast came, bowl of porridge and a nice piece of haddock. The time came to haul the nets again and the warps were knocked out of the block, by the watch. The rest of the crew put their wet gear on as the weather conditions were horrid with rain, sleet and a force 7 gale. The doors appeared, then the dan lenos appeared and it was apparent that half the trawl was missing and we scrambled the gear aboard. The word from the bridge, 'Change the trawl!'

The Mate stuck his head out the after doorway and said 'good luck' sarcastically and that I should have it fixed after his watch below. I BIT MY TONGUE.

All the crew went for breakfast. The cook sent a sandwich to the bridge with the Galley Boy and I went back in the mess deck. After the meal I told the lads my intentions. We left the mess deck and went back onto the deck.

When changing the trawl there is a lot of work to do as the shackles have to be reattach to the new trawl using either sharp knives or hacksaws to release the bobbins which have been attached with needles of twine. We lifted the cod ends first and lowered them on the port side. We had a bit of help with the wind and weather taking the net across but with the objects on the deck i.e., the washer and winch etc. the net kept getting caught. After about 30 minutes the net had been transferred across the spare net. To make things easier we put rope lashings every 8 feet apart and then threaded the Gilson wire through all the lashings. I asked the Skipper to turn the ship around to the weather side and when this was done, we heaved the net across which looked like a big sausage and lowered it down. We put the after Gilson wire on and then pulled the net into position. Finally, the last part of the operation we heaved the cod ends over to the fish pounds which we can sort out later.

I felt really pleased with myself as this was the first time that I had done this task. I attached the new net to the weights etc. and when completed, I was told to lift the trawl doors as we were going to another area. Finer ground, I hoped. Sent the watch on the bridge to steer the ship and lookouts. By this time the weather had calmed down. The rest of the crew helped sort the net out, pulling this way and that. to see what we could mend and what had to be replaced. We cut out the after top and lower wing. A spare one had been made and two men were attaching it back in place.

Myself and another person started to repair the square part of the net. When the nets are in the water, broken, sometimes it looks worse than it really is. The net took us nearly 2 hours to mend and we were about to put the net back safe when the Skipper shouted out the bridge. 'We will be shooting the net soon.' We secured the net and went aft for a quick cuppa and a smoke. The ship then eased down and we took our positions to put the net in the water. When the tasks were completed told the watch to start another top and lower wing and we will finish what's left to do in the afternoon. Team work is important at sea or in another work conditions.

We are now fishing at Fruholmen on the Norwegian Coast. Towing for two hours each tow. The first tow we had 60 baskets and the second tow 50 baskets. Steamed back to our start position. During lunch time I left the Mate in. The Skipper had his lunch and I had mine, back in the officer's mess. The Radio Operator gave the daily news that he had typed out. By 1300 hours the fish had been put away and we shot away the nets. There must have been about 20 ships in the area now all doing the same as us. Two, or maybe three hauls, then back to the starting gate and shot the net away.

I was then called to the bridge. The skipper asked what was going on between the mate and me. I said that I would let him know in dock. He said that he knew that something was not right but I thought it was not the time to tell him. He just said keep out of the Mates way. He then changed the subject and said; 'You can start by making another pair of cod ends.' I thought to myself 'My watchmates must really love me!'

Hauling time came upon us. The mate took charge of the deck and screamed at me for leaving him in at lunchtime. I just ignored him and bided my time. Pulling the net in at the rail using the 'lazy deckie', which is a line from the centre of the trawl belly, passed through a sleeve in the net. With a line attached through the centre of the headline it makes things much easier for both myself and 'knobhead' we are working the rail. You heave the 'lazy deckie' through a block on the bridge top and then you put a 'becket' around the net trap. The net at the rail then heaves up on the becket. The net was heaved up high then he sang out, 'lower the net' but the net had been trapped. The becket flew down and the link hit the Mates hand. He then went off the deck whilst we finished getting the net in with 50 baskets of large cod. We steamed back again and put the fish off the decks.

I popped down the fish room and we had a thousand kit, with another week to go. The Skipper called me on the bridge and asked: 'Do you want any flowers sending home.' My reply was: 'Yes and could I have a message saying 'Love and miss you. Love Ron.' He just shrugged his shoulders and said; 'By the way, you will have to stay up tonight whilst the mates hand goes.' down (SWELLING). He said that when we haul next time he would steam back and try and do a four-hour tow so that I can get some sleep.

We only had six more days before we were going home. We hauled at 1730 hours and steamed back during tea. Shot the net away at 1900 hours and then towed the net for four hours. The Mate relieved the Skipper for tea and I had mine. During tea the Skipper said: 'What's happened.' I said that the C link landed on his hand. When the word, 'All Square' came, I took off my gear and rolled in. I asked to be called 15 minutes before hauling time. I feel 'Knackered'.

Called out at 2230 hours hearing the words: 'Are you awake Bosun, hauling the nets in twenty minutes.' I reached down and put my thigh boots on and then my light jumper with no sleeves. I would cut the sleeves off any long-sleeved jumpers because there is nothing worse than having wet arms when working on the deck. I came out of my cabin and noticed the cook reading his book and said my pleasantries to him. The smell of stale bodies and sweaty socks, at times seemed overpowering and this was not helped by the liver house being at the stern of the ship. However, when the cook made fresh busters (buns) the smell seemed to disappear, although not for long. I went into the mess which was filled with smoke. Grey clouds floating in the air. We had a rule on the ships "no smoking an hour before meal times". I had a nice cup of tea made to the same recipe for many years. This recipe consisted of a tin large tea leaf, the size of clovers, 6 spoonsful of sugar mixed in a tin, (the size of a tin of beans at home). It had been put into a tea kettle with half a tin of evaporated milk. Tea was issued at 0700,1100, 1500, 1900 hours and if you wanted anymore you had to use what you obtained in the bond. I sat for a while, slowly waking up to the sound of the big hammer on the towing block. I went into the drying room and put on my wet gear, wrapped a muffler around my neck (scarf) and proceeded on to the deck.

I walked up to the winch and asked the watch who were guiding the warps; 'How much more warp is there to come up?' They shouted: '200 fathom.' Stood there, on the deck, finishing off my cigarette and looking skywards, watching the NORTHERN LIGHTS flicker across the sky with an array of colours. Quite mesmerising really. A full moon with its reflection on the sea for which people pay thousands to see. The marks on the warp come up: Shouted; 'LAST 50.' meaning last 50 fathoms. Then I heard: 'HOLD ON TO THE SHORT MARK!' This being the 25-fathom mark. The ship spun around to starboard and we were told to commence heaving the net.

The fore door came up first and a big chain was thrown through the door bracket which was then put onto a large hook which secured the door. The same process was repeated on the aft and as we started to heave on the bridles, we could see the cod ends beginning to appear. With a white plume of bubbles, the cod ends appeared and began to spread out with what seemed like a decent haul of fish. Bobbins then came aboard followed by the floats. We heaved slowly on the lazy deckie. Heaved it, nearly to the block and attached a rope becket around the belly of the net. We lowered the net and attached the becket to the G link which took the weight of the net. Called to the bridge to ask the Skipper if he would kick the engines astern, so that we can go forward and pick up the extension line to the lifting straps on the cod ends. We did this successfully four times, bringing in just the cod ends. By going astern each time, the cod ends were empty and just releasing and repeating the process. Finally, the last bag came aboard. I was told to lift the doors. Steaming back over the grounds once more to the starting point. The fish on the deck is estimated to be about 250 baskets, which is 150 kits of fish. I went on the bridge for the night rum, with orders: 'Don't give any to the mate, he is on painkillers.' I said: 'Don't worry, I won't.' As I'm going towards the lads on the deck, I had the Mates dram. Rollocks to him.

We hauled the nets at 0300 hours, with about 50 baskets of fish left on the deck from the previous haul. The mate had still not been on the scene and everything was going ok. The Northern Lights were still displaying their magical spectacle, along with shooting stars, far across the horizon which added to the scenery. Then, the same as last time, up popped the net with another deck load haul of fish, about 60 baskets. The net then went back into the water. After a quick smoke and cuppa, we went back to cleaning the fish. The mate was called to take the tow on the bridge with his injured hand, smirking out the bridge window as the crew are working. Sent a lad off the deck to clean and tidy the galley, as the cook will soon be getting up and he needed a clear start to his day, (don't want to upset the cook). We hauled the net just before breakfast with 50 baskets of fish. We then steamed back to the starting gate. The crew went aft for breakfast. I Had a nice piece of haddock with a couple of hot busters. After leaving the mess deck the mate came off the bridge and barged into me. My Response was, I ignored him as he was not going to provoke me!

Breakfast time the lads came of the deck and we took are wet gear off. We then went for breakfast which was a nice piece of haddock with a couple of hot busters and we all felt refreshed. Feeling happy. We all vacated the messdeck and a couple of the lads thanked the cook. Just got out of the mess and the mate deliberately barged into me. I just ignored him but just behind me had been Jerry, my watchmate, who had seen what the mate did. He quickly grabbed the mate by his throat and lifted the mate off the deck. He then dropped him on the deck like a lump of coal. He then bent down to the mate and muttered this is a warning: 'Leave the Bosun alone!' I then proceeded to the drying room and put my wet gear on, saying to Jerry: 'You shouldn't have done that.' He replied: 'I've seen what's been going on and I hope it stops now.' which it did. The Mate tried to be friendly but the damage had been done.

Back in the fish pounds normal banter returned and began to chat about going home soon. The fish had all been cleaned and we then washed down the decks. The Skipper then shouted out of the bridge window: 'Get a quick drink we will be shooting the trawl soon.' After a given time, we heard the engines ease down and proceeded to the deck. Tied the cod ends and remembering to thread the end in the bottom of the cod line. The weather at this time had been south westerly force 7. Put the yoyo hook into the cod end lifting chain then waited for the signal to put the net over, which duly came. Cod ends heaved over the rail the shout; 'Let go.' The rest of the net, the square, the belly and baiting then began to be pulled into the sea. The weight of the bobbins was lifted high. Then as the ship rolled, the order was given to lower them over the side which in turn had been quickly followed by the headline floats. I took my position behind the winch, and when ordered to I lower the dan lenos. Next went the trawl doors lowered down to the short mark of 25 fathoms. The ship then gathered speed and the order was to pay away the warps. We were shooting the nets away with a gale of wind, heavy spray from the sea with hailstones which felt like marbles hitting your face. 300 fathoms of warp went into the water. I then tapped on the winch barrel shouting: 'Last fifty.' The ship eased in and the amount of warp had been deployed. We then put the messenger hook and clipped it to the forward warp. The order was given; 'Let go of the messenger hook.' The winchman heaved on the messenger wire until it had been in position to secure in the towing block. When the securing pin had been put in place the messenger wire was then released, no order had come for all square, I then looked over the side as the trawl wires began to settle down, I then shouted up to the bridge: 'ALL SQUARE AFT.'

I was called to the bridge and was told by the Skipper that when we leave for home, we would be dropping the mate off in Honninsvag and a new mate will be joining us there. THE SKIPPER NOTICED A BIG SMILE ON MY FACE!!!

Finished gutting the fish and went aft to put my wets in the drying room. Had a quick cuppa and a smoke, went forward and in the fore hold finished off the cod ends. Was told not to put the cowhides on as they were going to be joined onto the belly and baiting's. The cow hides could be put on then. The ship was bouncing and shuddering and felt pleased that the cod ends were finished. The watch came forward to tell me that we would be hauling soon and to get a quick drink.

I was walking aft when a wave came flying over the rail which knocked me over and took my breath away. I hung on to the rail and then went aft. No damage done or so I thought. Eventually I got aft and went below to my cabin. I put on some dry gear. I took off my wet clothes and put them quickly in the shower with OMO wash powder and rinsed the soap suds off then. I hung them in the bathroom, had a quick smoke and a mouthful of tea.

I heard the towing block being knocked out. I took my position at the winch and then to the ships rail pulling in the net recovery operation. The cod ends came on board with about 50 baskets, 30 kit. Was just about to put the net back over and we heard the cry of 'WATER'. On hearing this word, we stop everything and got hold of something secure, handrails, winch etc. A large wave appeared on the ships rail but instead of the sea coming onboard, just the spray splashed everywhere. Skippered screamed; 'Get rid of the fish and we will shoot the net afterwards!'

I went aft, quick smoke and picked our gutting knives up. Then back into the fish pounds. Took us just over an hour then I was called onto the bridge. By this time the seas were enormous and you could hear the wind screaming through the rigging. Opened the bridge door and I was told to put a few lashings on the trawl, drop the doors in, batten down the hatches and to close all water tight doors. When we were laid you could hear the wind blowing and a spray of water now and again but the Queen was a good sea ship. We worked as a team. After door in first, lashed the after end down and secured with the after Gilson. We then went to the fore door and did the same. Tied the cod ends to the winch bollard, used the foreword Gilson and halving becket to tie the net down. By this time the men in the fish room had finished. With a bit of banter from big Jerry, saying:

'You can come up now, the works all done.' Everyone laughed because no one is going to disagree. I went aft and made sure everyone was accounted for. The liver man, Jerry, said; 'Shall I do the livers' The answer was: 'No Jerry wait until the weather abates.'.

I went on the bridge and told the Skipper that everyone was now off the deck. He sent me down with the rum and smiled: 'Who is having the mate's dram?' I just smirked at him and said; 'I'm sharing it each time I dish it out.' Which was the TRUTH. I dished the rum out and by the time I got back to the bridge it was nearly lunchtime. To my surprise the Skipper said: 'I know what's been going on and like I said before, keep away from him. That was my CUE to have my meals in the messdeck. Forecast for our area NORTHELY. STORM FORCE 10, with heavy SNOWFALL. At least it will give me time to get my washing dry.

Weather outside was atrocious. Ship rolling this way and that. Hearing the sound of the wind and the crashing sounds of water coming on board. Big pan of shackles had been the order of the day for lunch time. I went onto the bridge just after 1100 hours for the morning dram. I was then told that we would be docking tomorrow in Honninsvag, picking up the new mate and dropping the old one off. This it would be about lunchtime and the pilots had been ordered. I came off the bridge and informed the crew. There were smiles and the crew looked happy. It had not been a hard trip as such but I learned a lot about myself and how this trip soon passed by. It could have been better if the mate had not been such a prat. Still had a couple of days to steam home and it would be nice to be able to be steady again when we get to the fjords. A red-hot shower was the order of the day.

Came off watch at tea time and we are now back on steaming watches. Enjoyed my tea cowpie, mash, peas with a thick gravy. I noticed that the Galley Boy had been crying and asked what was wrong. He told me something about the mate and his mother and that he could be his son. How low can you get, upsetting a 16-year-old. My advice was; 'Don't believe him and keep away from him. He is going home tomorrow. He then seemed to settle down a bit. I left it like that and staggered to my bed hoping that I had done the thing right with the advice I gave to the young lad. Called out at 0245 hours for watch. The ship seemed a little steadier. I drank my tea, had a quick smoke and then went onto the bridge. The Skipper pulled me aside and asked about the galley boy. I told him my version of what had happened and the advice I had given him. But apparently the mate had had another go at him and the skipper had a visit from the cook and he said the same as me. The Skipper said; 'Thanks for letting me know.' It was left like that or so I thought!!!

Skipper gave me the watch orders and told to keep a good look out. The weather had begun to ease. When the skipper closed his cabin door my watchmate asked if I would like a pot of special tea making. It's what we bought out of the bond and the reply, of course, was 'yes please'. He returned 10 minutes later and said: 'It's all sorted with the mate.' I asked: 'What do you mean? I didn't realise that we had been talking out loud,' He said; 'I warned him a few days ago.' Big Jerry to the rescue! I came off watch at breakfast and smirking at me was the mate, sitting in the officer's mess with a lovely black eye and a swollen lip. He then walked away from me and muttered: 'This isn't finished yet.'

Sat down to breakfast with the lads, the deckie had the Mates watch. The person in charge had been a thirdhand

and he had sailed with my father in-law a few times. The Mate was packing his gear. The weather by this time had been a southerly 3 to 4 with heavy snow squalls. We had about 20 miles to run in to Honninsvag. I went to lay laid down and soon fell asleep. I awoke about 1100 hours and went on the bridge and took the morning dram round to the crew. LAST ONE. for the trip. I was told that we would be tying up to the quay at 1230 hours. The time duly arrived. The ropes on the were on quayside which were secured to the ship. Kaara the agent came aboard first, soon followed by the pilots and you guessed it KBS was back. The daymen, with the fish room man, went down the fish room and secured it for passage home. I went on the deck and cleaned the cod ends out with the deckie learner. The fish room was soon finished. A basket of mixed fish had been brought up in ice for the crews' meals. The hatches were then sealed. The Skipper shouted down that the new mate was coming about 1900 hours tonight. The agent took the knobhead off [MATE] and not one of the crew spoke or gave him a hand to take his gear off the ship.

Prior to tea time all the deck and equipment had been stowed on deck. We then put away the fish washer and secured it on the deck. Just as we finished the skies opened up with heavy snow, settling very quickly. I went off the deck and sat in the officer's mess and enjoyed my tea. Both the pilots were filling their faces with fish and saying; 'Very good cook.' Eating it like there was no tomorrow. 1930 hours the taxi pulled up with the new Mate, Tommy Pembroke. Minutes later the shout from the bridge: 'LET GO FORWARD, LET GO AFT.' and we left Honninsvag. HOMEWARD BOUND. It had been a long day but I was back on watch again until 2300 hours. Looking forward to some SHUTEYE.

The new Mate popped up and introduced himself to the Skipper and signed on to the log book. I had a quick yarn to him and he asked what happened to the other mate. I told him he had hurt his hand hauling the net and during a gale of wind, he lost his balance and slipped in the bathroom chuckle chuckle. The Mate asked; 'Why did you need him for just going home with the ship'. I just said that we had lost a couple of days fishing due to bad weather and that he was needed. It just goes to show that we have just got rid of the old mate and the atmosphere on the ship had been lifted. Everyone knew that we would be home soon and feeling happy. KBS told us to be quiet whilst he manoeuvred the ship through a narrow channel in the fjords. The mate whispered: 'I will speak later.' Which we did. As he opened the bridge door you could smell the aroma of foo foo powder and aftershaves with the crews able to have showers and time off, now that the trawling part had finished but we still had lots to do.

Watch had brought up a nice pot of 'special tea'. We had left Honninsvag nearly 2 hours ago. The pilot had just been talking on the ships radio to one of his colleagues. He came off the radio and said that the airport in Honninsvag was closed because of snow drifts and high winds. Does that mean the mate is not going home then - ha-ha? The Mate Tommy Pembroke came up early and said that he would take over the watch. I gave him our position on the chart and left the watch to the mate. I left the bridge with a smile on my face and went into the mess for a quick cup of 'Rosie lee' with a nice fish sarnie and a smoke. I then went to roll in and had a quick read of the Grimsby telegraph which the mate had thrown on my bunk. I then read a little of what was happening at home. I must have fallen asleep - absolutely exhausted.

Woke up just before breakfast with newspaper over my face and my bunk light still on. Slowly climbed out of my bunk, took my jumper off the radiator and put my clumpers on (cut down wellingtons). I sat on my seat locker having a quick smoke. The watchman came down to call the watch. I climbed the ladder into the officer's mess. The Galley Boy asked if I wanted any fried eggs and bacon this morning or fish for my breakfast. 'Fish' was my answer which came straight out of the frying pan. Plenty of salt and vinegar, with a hot buster. Still taste it. even to this day I have some form of fish for breakfast as well but not every day. Most fisherman, do if the truth be told. The Pilot, KBS came in for breakfast, duly sat down and had a platter of fish alongside him. that he was weighing up for himself. Nearly time for my watch. I waited for my watch mates and then went up together to the bridge. We took over the watch and the Skipper went down for his breakfast with the other Pilot, Pieter when KBS had relieved him.

We were now approaching Tromso Bridge. Weather force 3 to 4 with light snow. Just clear of the bridge and we passed the Vivaria going north and he called us up. I told him that the 'old man' had gone to breakfast and would be up soon. The Skipper came up and spoke to the Vivaria from the wireless room. Foreman daymen came up and asked for the bridge mats so that they could be cleaned. Duly took them up and gave the deck a quick sweep. As we were steaming through the fjords, we could see the houses and chalets on the shoreline and noticed all the bright colours of the roofs which were easy to see in the snow-covered landscape. Went into the radio room to send a telegram home, to let my wife know we were on our way home. The father-in-law said that he had already spoken to the mother-in-law to let them know. The rest of the watch soon past and lunchtime soon came upon us. Lovely roast venison with all the trimmings, followed by treacle duff. Oh, the joys! KBS, sat alongside me with a large plate of FISH. Passed the fish room man going to the bridge as the Skipper wanted the fish room tally which was 1,700 kits mase up of 1,200 cod 300 haddock 100 coley, 200 mixed. Hoping to turnout 1,800.

We dropped KBS and Pieter off on to the pilot boat at Lodigen in the Lofton islands. Now bound Grimsby. I am really looking forward to seeing the wife and children. It seems ages ago since we sailed from there but, we are only 18 days away. It will be 20 days to docking. The trip has not gone without some hitches but generally I am pleased with my first trip as Bosun.

My father-in-law has taught me lots of things and I will always be grateful to him. It would have been a lot better without all the stress from the mate but I think that in general I held it together. Just sitting in the mess with the lads and having a game of cards. Everyone is in a good mood and just going to have another half hour playing cards then having some shut eye.

We have been steaming for nearly 24 hours since we left Lodigen (Norway) and are now approaching Flamborough Head. The last meal of the trip and its dinner time, so I had better get something to eat. This morning I had been cleaning my cabin, bit of soogey woogey. I don't think it has been cleaned for a while, as such, but some people are cleaner than others. All carpets have been laid down. The daymen had been down the fish room to bring some fish up for going home which then had then been filleted, then shared out equally. Dinner had been spam, eggs and chips, with yesterday's bread. I then went onto the bridge with my watchmates and relieved the mate and took over the watch. Nice to see other trawlers chasing for the tide and jockeying for position for the fish market. Just after 1500 hour we came around the light ship. The watch had been sent down below whilst I took the helm in the river. We were soon approaching the fish docks. The Brenda Fisher came and took our head ropes whilst the Alfred Bannister took the stern ropes, both were TUGBOATS. They then took us in to the fish docks.

Passing through the lock gates I caught a glimpse of my wife (Cheryl], alongside her uncle Fred. When the ropes were all secured, the Skipper told me to leave the wheel midships and that my job was done. He popped down to his cabin, told me that I did well this trip and said that I still had things to learn. He then gave me a bottle of whiskey (maybe Chivas Regal?) and that is when I fell in love with the blend. I went down below, picked up my kitbag and my bass of fish, climbed the ships rail to get ashore. I saw the wife on the pontoon and went over to her put the bottle into her handbag. I gave her a quick kiss and then we went to the car. We arrived home to the wife's auntie who was babysitting the children. I took a fry of fish to the local chip shop and enjoyed our tea. After tea watched a bit of telly and a shout came from upstairs telling me that the bath had been run for me. I had my bath, went down for a cigarette, and then it was time for bed. Every time we dock it feels like a honeymoon and its good night once more until landing day.

Landing Day I woke up about 0800 hours feeling relaxed. Had a full English breakfast, bacon, eggs, sausages, tinned tomato [with oxo] toast and fried bread. I always felt spoilt when I came home. After breakfast, the wife dropped me off at Billy Raymond's (hairdressers) for a haircut and a shave with a cut throat razor. I had a steady walk home, bathed and suited. The wife had a hair appointment for later in the day and had arranged a babysitter.

l left the house about 1100 hours to have a quick pint in the Clee Park (pub). I duly walked in and ordered a pint and had a quick look around. In the corner I could see Harold, Sid and Bernard Brennan and I also saw a couple of the Carters. There was also a couple standing at the bar who I did not know. I downed my pint, ordered another. drank it and went outside to jump into a taxi. I then went down dock and paid the taxi fare. A couple of the crew were already at the office. The time was now approaching 1230 hours. Bill Battie and Charlie Ward were both in the office and both said that I had a good report from the Skipper, [surprise, surprise] and said that the other mate had come home but would not be going back as Pemmy was going with us.

We turned out 1,750 kits and made £24,500. Really pleased with myself and picked up quite a lot of money [compared to deckie] £170 including tax rebate. I picked up my fry of fish, dropped it into Billy Raymond's, to pick up later in the day. I had a pint in the Humber and saw Harry Scotter, Billy Jones, Bobby Elliot all stood at the wicket. I went into the Hitching Rail and had a quick drink with Jerry Proudlove, with his lovely wife Rose. Left there to go in the Corporation and saw all the regulars, Steve Rodger, Billy Wako, Syd Dillon, Smithy, Trouser Nell, Nuf Nuf Ann, Frank Hargreaves and Killer Cook. Just leaving the pub and passed Tommy Smith and exchanged a few words as I was leaving to meet the wife at 1400 hours in Marks and Sparks. I found her in the car park waiting in the car. We did a bit of shopping AND then popped into the White Bear and had another pint followed by dinner in the Pea Bung. Left after the meal and popped to the bank to put the money in.

I collected the fish from the hairdressers, then went home and chilled out for a while. I took my suit off and laid down on the couch.

At 1900 hours the father-in-law picked us both up as we had planned to go for a meal which was going to be my treat. We went to the Splash near Louth with the mother-in-law (Nelly), Tracy and Billy [Cheryl's, brother and sister]. Sirloin steaks, fillet steaks, chicken were the mains ordered for the meal. The father-in-law passed me the wine list and I looked at the list. He ordered off the list and I just grimaced after seeing the price. It was a lovely meal followed by desserts, cheese board and coffees to finish. The waitress asked if we had finished and I asked for the bill. Unbeknown to me the father in-law had already paid it and she said it was taken care of. What a wind up! That was when I knew I was part of the family. During the meal nothing had been said about the trip. Driving home the father-in-law said; 'I will pick you up tomorrow and take you to the bond stores.' which he did with plenty of freebies for the family. Popped into the office and picked up my oil money (cod livers that we saved). The next day visiting the family and the following day we sailed again - 3-day millionaires. Would I do it again - the answer is YES!

9

Northern Queen – Iceland

Down for sailing 0900 hours. I woke up at 0700 hours as the taxi pick-up was 0800 hours. A quick visit to the bathroom and then downstairs to put the kettle on. I then placed my kitbag alongside the front door. I made a nice pot of tea, lit another smoke and then it begins - clock watching 0750 hours then 0755 and then into the front room looking for the taxi. 0800 hours and the taxi has still not arrived. Have they forgotten about me? I ask myself. Another cigarette then pacing up and down in the room 0810 hours and still no taxi. Then I see it pulling up on my front. I go to open the door and put my bag outside. I then pop upstairs to say my goodbyes. It gets harder when you have a woman and child that you love. Kiss the baby, says goodbye to the wife but she follows me downstairs. I give her a final hug and a kiss and we say goodbye to each other. Both secretly wandering in our minds whether I will come home safely. I then climbed in the taxi and we travel straight down dock. I noticed the general public going about their daily business. Taking the children to school, shopping or just going to work. My choice of work is to be a TRAWLER MAN!

Arrived on the docks, got out of the taxi and picked my bag up. I climbed the steep ladders onto the bow of the ship then stepped across the breakwater then off the whaleback towards the after accommodation. I stepped inside to the great smell of the liver house which sometimes churns your stomach over. I finally arrived into my cabin and put my clean gear and goodies away. I noticed a new face and he introduced himself as Harold Botte, who turned out to be a plain cook but the food was rather tasty, just like grannies. I said hi to the rest of the crew, then went ashore to pick my new bedding from Vincent's. I gave that smirky faced thing behind the counter my chit and he duly passed me it over the counter. It consisted of a blanket, pillow and mattress. I unrolled the bedding and just took the mattress with me then I was asked what else did I want. told him to piss off as he tried to make me pay twice previously. I popped into Coleridge's and picked up a few items I needed reading, colour magazines, (flower arranging), a couple of tins of old Holborn and a tin of petrol with a packet of flints and my last item was a Fray Bentos pie. I chucked my mattress on to the whaleback then climbed aboard. I had just made a nice drink of coffee, when the mate came into the galley and said that I was wanted on the bridge. I took my drink with me and proceeded to the wheelhouse. The Skipper [father in-law] told me to standby the wheel and we were pulled out of the dock by the Brenda Fisher (tug). All clear of the lock gates the tug let go and the Skipper shouted thanks Bernard. We left Grimsby astern of us going on a new adventure, man versus fish.

Both tugs have left us and we are now approaching the burcom (river buoy) and passing port to port with the Northern Reward, who looked pretty full. The Skipper waved at the Reward's Skipper, Mick George, I believe and we sailed on towards the next buoy. Hailed Sand and Bull Fort both standing alone with circular frames. Passing the Bull Buoy now heading to the Spurn Light Ship and after passing the Light Ship the course was set to north and half west. Looks like we are bound for Iceland. I was then told to get the daymen on the deck and after lunch told to give them a hand. Back to normal and we are just an hour out of dock. Lunch time approached and we are passing Easington with its large masts, highlighting the hillside. Now we could see Filey and Scarborough Head just ahead of us. The course was set to pass about 3 miles off the land and we are going up a Decca Lane 21.5c but would be pleased when we are going the other way.

Lunch time came and daymen were told to go on the deck after lunch. A few moans came from them apparently but that is the normal thing. Pemmy relieved me and I handed my watch over. I went below to get my lunch and saw the foreman daymen. I told him to be on the deck for quarter past one. Lunch soon passed and I asked the Skipper if I could take the deckie learner on watch with me as the weather's calm and he can learn how to steer the ship. It's the lad's 5th trip to sea and he has not had the chance as yet. The Skipper said that this was fine but only until we get near the fishing grounds, in about 50 hours.

After lunch changed into my working gear and the first thing, we did was to lower the yoyo davit and then to put the washer up as the seas were calm. I was told to take the old bridles off the winch which we did and placed them on the starboard side. One by one we put them over the starboard quarter and released them over the side, making sure nobody was in the area. Wee then put up went the gratings and pound boards, along with the jockey boards with metal clamps to keep them in place. 1500 hours and we all went for a quick cuppa.

The mate was told to put 50 fathom bridles onto the winch which we did when returning to the deck. I lifted the cod ends using the yoyo and Gilson wire to open them up. Climbed inside then gave them the once over. The cod line meshes needed replacing, so I climbed out of the net, opened the bottom, cut out the old meshes out and replaced them with new ones. Teatime soon approached which was a lovely mixed grill consisting of steak, sausage, ham, fresh fried tomatoes, egg and jockey whips with apple crumble, custard to follow. Quick smoke on the deck, seeing Newcastle and North Shields on our port beam. I then went and rolled in. On watch again at 2300 hours. Feeling knackered already and its only day one.

Rolled in after tea but it was a waste of time. A few of the lads had a few beers and were singing at the top of their voices; Nelly Dean, I Remember you, etc. Then the record player came out and they were playing Twist and Shout, Waterloo Sunset, Build Me Up Buttercup and Oh My Love, My Darling, I hunger for your love. It was ok until the batteries started to run low. Bridge watch came to call my gang out and told them not to call the deckie learner out. He can come on watch tomorrow dinnertime.

Whilst climbing up the stairs, the Galley Boy was standing there as white as a ghost and he had just been sick again. He will just have to get used to it for now. When I started, I had been lucky but I think it was working the waltzes in my school holidays and getting used to balancing etc. My watchmates looked a bit rough and I think they had been partying. I had a can before I rolled in but didn't want any more as I was a watchkeeper and I wanted to give a good impression especially as my father-in-law was the Skipper. I relieved the watch and we were just about to cross the Moray Firth.

The weather had freshened since this afternoon southerly 6, clear skies and to port we could see the loom of the land and flickering lights from other ships in the distance. My watchmate asked if I would take the wheel then opened the door and all I could hear was the sound of Huey and Ralph. He then reappeared smelling of sick and I told him to go and get himself sorted out. He came back with a pot of special from last trips bond. Big Jerry took the wheel off me and said that his wife (Rose) liked me and thought I was a gentleman. I think that he had been the hardest man in Grimsby but was terrified of his wife.

I went on the boat deck and read the ships speed from the watch face and we were doing a good 10.5 knots. The phosphorus, leaving a trail of light as the propellor churned the sea up behind us. Pleased to get back onto the bridge as there was a nip in the air. The cook must be up as I can smell fresh bread. Most fisherman wouldn't eat supermarket bread because they have been spoilt by having fresh bread every day. The watch soon passed and Jerry went down to call the watch and daymen. He came back and said that the new daymen [Terry B] said to tell you to fuck off. I said to call him again at 0715 hours, which he did. He then told me that he was out of his bed now. Jerry pulled him out and told him that you don't speak about the Bosun like that. In later years if Jerry ever saw me, he always said that he would look after me. I often saw him ashore and he always looked well dressed with a suit and tie. Soon the Mate came up to relieve me with his watch and I gave him all the information. I signed off on the Log Book and Radio Log and sat in the messdeck having my breakfast. Foreman dayman reported to the Mate for his orders.

Called out for my bond 1130 hours 5 tins of Old Friend,10 packets of fag papers, 2 packets of Typhoo Tea,12 Mars bars 1 bottle of Kiora orange juice, 2 tins Quality Street, 6 tins of milk, 400 Benson cigarette's and given 6 tins of red bass. I put all these in my pillowcase and was just about to leave when I was asked; 'Don't you want this nogging of rum'. I went straight off the bridge and I put my bond away. I had my lunch, mince and taties with brown sauce and a fresh buster. After lunch 1330 hours went on the deck and noticed a couple of bobbins had split and were duly replaced together with the footropes that needed new spacers. Just approaching Aberdeen and there are quite a few ships about. The deckie learner has gone on watch with the deckies and I'm sure they will let him have a go at steering the ship. Titch and I started to overhaul the trawl whilst the other two went down the fish room to get it sorted for when we start fishing.

1500 hours went aft for a cuppa and a scone then back to the deck to finish overhauling the rest of the net. Nearly tea time so I went off the deck and had a quick shower. I sat down for my tea, steak, (bit tough) chips, peas and carrots followed by a treacle duff and custard. Loosened my belt. Then onto the bridge for watcho. Just abeam of Rattary Head and now the course is set towards Duncansby Head and the Pentland Firth. The skipper decided to go through it with the tide and wind being in our favour. The Skipper left orders that he wanted to be up when we were approaching Duncansby. There seemed to be a lot of ships about and not all obeying the rules of the sea, so keeping alert. The watch went down to make a nice pot of special which duly arrived with a handful of biscuits which I declined with still being full from teatime. Had a little show with the Northern Lights but then the sky became overcast. 2245 hours the Mates watch was called and they came onto the bridge. We were nearing Duncansby Head and the Mate called the Skipper. My gang went aft. and closed all the water tight doors. A quick smoke in the mess then went down to my pit to sleep which didn't take long to do.

Called for breakfast and the watch. I had a full English breakfast with all the trimmings. Walked past the messdeck and saw Terry B. with a lovely shiner. I then went up on to the bridge and took over the watch, Passed Dunnet Head at

1230 hours so made good time coming through the Pentland Firth. Jerry took over the steering and looked at me just smiling. I asked him what was funny and he said that Terry B. had been mouthing me off so he stumbled into his fist. The Skipper rolled out at 9ish and sent me back on the deck with the daymen who had started to make top and lower wings up, as spares.

I gave them a hand and the Skipper shouted to me that the mast light had just blown. Popped on the bridge and asked have you checked the fuse first, not like last time. The power to the light had been turned off and up I climbed with a fair wind behind me. I duly climbed the mast, replaced the bulb, shouted down and given the ok. I climbed down the mast when a shout came off the bridge telling me that I could have a dram for doing it. But there was a catch, he gave me the morning issue which I dished out without an extra one for the climbing. What a crafty man!

I went back on the bridge just before lunch and filled the log book in, no need for the radio log which the operator did during the day. Smoked fish or cow pie had been on the menu for lunch and I opted for the pie. I went on the deck for a smoke and the Smyrll was just passing us heading for the Faroe, Islands. It was a passenger and general cargo boat, running from Denmark, Aberdeen, Lerwick, Faroes and then to Iceland on weekly turnaround. We must be nearing land as a few gulls were now appearing. Many a time you couldn't see them for miles but as soon as you put the waste food over the side, they suddenly appeared. Just over the horizon, about 20 miles away, I could see the Faroe Islands in the distance. We should be fishing around breakfast time. Rolled in for an hour and started to read my flower magazines and think of home. Oh, how I love Gardening lol.

After a couple of hours sleep, popped on the deck and put a new cod line into the cod ends. I went for tea, pizzas or sausages chips beans, followed by a Manchester tart. Finished tea and had a quick smoke then a game of cards. Rummy first and then a game of Cribb whilst listening to radio Luxembourg, until watch time.

Went on watch at 2300 hours, and did a 4-hour watch which had been uneventful, apart from the dancing lights flickering in the sky with the occasional shooting star. I passed the watch over to the Mate at 0300 hours, then rolled in. Called out at 0700 hours with the watch saying we would be shooing just after breakfast. I, went into the Officer's Mess had an egg and bacon banjo with a couple of loose sausages, quickly followed by a nice cuppa.

The Mate came off the bridge and was just about to start his breakfast, when the ship eased her speed and then stopped. Told the Mate to have his meal as I would put the net over which he did and then went below with his watchmates. Fishing watches were then set. We put the after door over the rail, followed by the fore door and put the yo yo hook into the coded lifting point. The order then came to heave them out followed shortly afterwards by 'LET GO!' The net soon followed, then the bobbins and floats were thrown over. The engines were engaged and the dan lenos were lowered. I took my place near the forward winch break, lifted the forward. door off its safety chain and the same with the after door. Order came 'Lower the Doors!' Then as the ship gathered speed, the order came 'AWAY THE WARPS!' This is where we opened the breaks and keeping on the tension whilst watching the marks being counted. Then came the final marks and shouting to the bridge, 'Last

50!' Meaning the number of fathoms left to go in the water. The ship eased down its speed whilst the messenger wire had been attached to the forward warp which when released pulled the two warps, forward. and aft, together into the towing block and the shout 'All square!' came from aft. This meant we are now on our first tow of the trip.

We were fishing at a place called the 'Whaleback'. The net had been in the water for two and a half hours when the net was pulled back on board containing 40 baskets mixed fish. Ling, skate, reds and a few large cod. The order was to put the net over again which we did. After gang shouted 'ALL SQUARE!' I was then given the morning dram to dish out. The fish was nearly all cleaned before lunch and we let the mates watch in. After lunch I had been called on the bridge to take the next tow which was hauled after a 4 hours tow with a hundred baskets. Again, mixed fish but more rough fish than prime. Prime being haddock and cod. Teatime came and I went onto the bridge whilst the Skipper went for his tea and in turn, I did the same. I then went for my watch below.

Most trawlermen would go back to sea tomorrow. We are a special breed of men who have known hardships and good times. With the hardships comes STRENGTH. With good times comes HAPPINESS. We all liked a drink. Sometimes a scrap (fight). Whilst at sea we were all part of a team who looked after each other, remaining friends for life. Such was the bond together.

We broke the belly on the trawl and the Skipper said: 'Drop the doors in. We are steaming to the Cape!' We were ordered to keep the fishing watches going. Should be at the grounds in 15 hours which will be mid-morning. Repaired the net and lashed the trawl down ready for passage. Don't know whether it is just me but the weather seems to be getting colder. Time for some tea and a bit of shut eye. We are now starting to roll a bit. Best get comfy and wedged up for the night and get my gardening magazine out again.

Been steaming most the night and just been called for breakfast. We had our first fried fish for our meal and a bowl of porridge. The Mate came off the bridge saying that we will be shooting the nets about 0900 hours and to change the 60 fathom bridles and put the 40s on and to cut the 60s down to 50 fathoms. I thought things were going too smoothly. I pulled the bridles off and flaked them on the port side and put the 40s on. 0900 hours came and we shot the nets over the side.

Looking around there must be about thirty ships in the area. The after-door men shouted; 'All square!'. We then all proceeded aft for a quick smoke and to take my wets off. Ten minutes later we cut down the first bridle, measured the eye then tied it down and took the turns out. Big Johnny Walker held the batten. I then began putting the spike in 3, 2, 1, then turn over to complete. This took nearly an hour and then did the same to the other bridle. We just finished the second one when the order came for hauling time. The nets have only been in the water for two hours. There were a few moans coming from the mess. When the order came; 'Knock out' and we started hauling the nets again. The doors came up and swung round to starboard, to take a turn out of her. Then as the dan leno's came up, the cod ends came up as well. We pulled the net in and used the winch to do all the hard work. When we had finished, we had about a hundred baskets (60 kits). It's a good start. Put the nets over and all square for 1145 hours. Took the morning dram around and lunch time was upon us.

The Skipper said he was not going for lunch and to go and get mine. Pemmy (Mate) asked whether I had started the bridles? I replied that they were finished. 'Did I do them properly?' He asked. I just shrugged my shoulders. After lunch we were back in the fish pounds to clean the fish. We just finished the fish and the shout came; 'Hauling time' and another hundred baskets came on board. We are 21 miles off the North Cape fishing.

The Galley Boy came along to give us a hand gutting. I told him to put his hand into the fishes' gill, then get his knife and cut across the nape, to then take the knife right down its belly and whilst cutting down to cut the livers out and throw them into a basket. The fish then had to be 'chucked' [thrown] in the washer. The process had to be repeated until all the fish were cleaned and off the deck. I think he tried a couple of times then threw his hand in.

We hauled before tea – about 50 baskets. Shot the net away again and relieved the Skipper for tea. He came back shortly after with just a fish sarnie and told me to get mine and in the same breath; 'You've done well today.' I tucked into a nice steak and onion pie, with all the trimmings which was followed by bread-and-butter pudding. Feeling tired so didn't bother with the gardening magazine. Crawled into bed and it's lights out.

Called out at midnight as the trawl had come fast and we lost the belly lengtheners and cod ends. The spare trawl was now being used and I am glad that I had made the new pair of cod ends a few days ago. Left Richard Hardy to join on the new net with Johnny Walker. My task was to put new cowhides on - 3 half and 5 full. Fitted the new cod line, lashed the trawl down and tied it to the rail. I didn't realise how cold it had become but it was ok if working but now the cold was hitting me. The winchman said; 'Pee on your hands - it will get the circulation going but don't run them under a tap!'

The Skipper is now watch below and the mate called me on the bridge saying we will be getting our cod ends back during the day. Someone made a name for himself by going across other ships sterns. Had my nogging of rum with my watch then into the mess to get warm. The hot aches then hit me and lasted a few minutes but then abated. Hauled the nets at 0330 hour with 60 baskets of large cod. This was easy to gut and put away. Sent big Jerry to tidy the galley in preparation for the cook. We don't want to upset HIM.

Fish all put away prior to breakfast. I had my food in the crews' mess and I had what looked like a boil on my left arm which is now beginning to hurt and feeling heavy. I will show the Skipper later in the day. We hauled at 0730 hours and the Skipper is now on the bridge. With another 50 baskets of fish and without naming names, a vessel came alongside us and dropped our cod ends into the sea with flotations on it which we managed to get on board. We would repair the damage when time allows. The weather began to blow from the north east with ice now forming. 0845 hours the net had been in the water and at 0900 hours the net came fast. Both the doors came up, then the dhan lenos, then all looked well but when we began to pull the net in by hand, we discovered weight in the net. Slowly but surely the net had been pulled up and a Stolberg stomper was discovered in the net.

We lifted the cod end on board, undid the cod line and lowered the net onto the deck. We then opened the cod ends to release the rock and were told to make ready to put the rock back over using the Gilson wire, large crocodile spanner and the yoyo. We took the hook off the wire, wrapped it around the rock and put the yoyo wire into the Gilson wire shackle, heaved it up and pulled slowly on the yoyo until the rock was over the side. We heaved on the yo yo and slackened the Gilson and the rock fell back into the sea. Five minutes later we put the net back over the side and commenced fishing. I took the rum round and Jerry said that I could have his and before I had finished taking it around, I had mine. Took the bottle back to the bridge and we were among the ice flows drifting down from the North. Not all the crew have seen the ice before now.

0400 hours and halfway from finishing the fish. We heard a high pitch screeching sound as the trawl warps were being pulled back into the sea. We had come fast. The Mate was on the bridge and he had stopped the ship. We had started heaving on the warps but we were hard and fast. The weather had been North Easterly 6, with light icing, as we are heaving heavy water is coming on board with the crew having to hold on to something secure, i.e., handrails and fixtures. I could feel the icy water on my face and my beard was beginning to ice up. After about 20 minutes the warps came free and we started to bring the doors up and the rest followed shortly after. Heaved the net by hand but then discovered a big hole in the belly's and 30 baskets of fish.

We started to repair the nets. It was that cold I couldn't feel my hands and it didn't help having the water spray and pitching of the vessel. Just about finished the net when from the bridge we heard the sound of 'WATER', being shouted by the Mate. We instantly stopped mending the nets and grabbed the handrails, just as the water came on board which took me off my feet. The water subsided and I stood up with both boots full of water. The rest of my clothes were wet through. Three other members of the crew had been knocked over by the wave. I shouted up to the Mate that we were going to get changed which we did.

I chucked my clothes in my cabin and put dry clothing on. I stood up to roll a cigarette and then I started shaking like a leaf. I used about 4 cigarette papers but all were wet through. The cook saw me struggling and rolled a fag for me. All the crew had followed me off the deck and we went back on together. The Mate came off the bridge and told us to get our breakfast and we would put the nets back after we have all eaten. A bowl of porridge finished by a nice fish sarnie and a cuppa. We later went back on the deck and put the net in the water. A quick drink and returned into the fish pounds. The fish, by this time, were half frozen and the texture felt like cardboard. It took a little longer to complete the task but we finally finished the fish.

I popped on the bridge to show the Skipper my fore arm which had doubled in size since yesterday and was now very painful. I was told to get the Mate up on the bridge to look at my arm. He said it needed lancing so the medical locker had been opened with items needed. I stood near the bridge chair and laid my hand down and the mate told me to look away from my hand. He then used a scalpel and pierced my skin. It felt like an eruption as the poison reached the deckhead of the bridge. Thick poison came out of the wound and pressure had to be applied to remove the rest. The relief from the pain was immediate. The Skipper initially said it was only a boil but in actual fact it had been a carbuncle. The wound was lathered in iodine and dressed but I was then sent back on the deck.

During the morning the seas were becoming less, with a southerly wind forecast in the offing. We were still working the ice field which was now about 30 miles off Isa fjord. We were towing alongside small ice floats that sometimes hit the ships sides which could be heard down below. Fishing was good with plenty of boats averaging 50/60 baskets for three-hour tows. My arm felt much easier now and I was now pain free. Most of us had a chance to have a cat nap –

40 winks sleep - when we were called again for hauling time. The bit of ice that had been on the ship had nearly all gone, with brilliant sunshine thawing it rapidly. The trawl came up uneventfully. 70 baskets of cod which we pulled aboard with the halving becket. It came aboard ok but broke a couple of cod line meshes which were soon rectified. Put the net over and the order came; 'ALL SQUARE'. First time that Richard Hardy had been at the towing block and the words of 'All Square' was shouted. Richard thanked me letting him block up but that would be his new area of working - after door man. Went on the bridge for the morning dram and promptly told off saying that it had been too much for the cod ends and next time split the fish. Took his advice then vacated the bridge.

All the lads were either in the fish pounds or down the fish room. I had just about reached the fish pounds when I heard the galley boy Eric, shouting for me with panic in his voice. He stood trembling and I asked; 'What's the matter'. He told me, with a shaky voice, that he had been helping the cook grind the meat with the mincing machine. This was a machine that was clamped on to the work surface, with lumps of meat put into a hole, the handle was turned like an organ. It would churn the meat through a tube and then come out as minced meat. Eric was using the handle to turn the machine but he turned away to look at someone passing by just as the cook poked his index finger into the machine and the tip of his finger came off into the mincer. I went on to the bridge to inform the Skipper and asked if I could use the tubular bandage and adapter to dress the wound which we did successfully. I went back into the fish pounds and carried on gutting. I told the lads why I had been absent.

Halibut soup was on the lunchtime menu, with fresh bread buns (busters) which were delicious. We hauled the net again after lunch. The Mate was now in control at the winch. I then shouted; 'Door coming up.' But he acted a little slow and when the door came up it made one hell of a noise. The Skipper shouted: 'BE CAREFUL.' It is a good job we were not standing by the chain as this time it would have killed someone. The rest of the procedure for lifting the trawl went unhindered and another 60 baskets of fish. We took about one hour to finish gutting the lovely large cod. Clearing the washer, the Mate shouted; 'Somebody drop down here and give us a hand.' I jumped down shovelling a bit of ice and laying some fish whilst the Mate had a fag. I had a good look around and we had around a thousand kit on board. Had a haul mid-afternoon with another 40 baskets of fish. Cleared the fish and was told to turn the washer around. Now teatime was upon us, with mince pie being on the menu. Needless to say, nobody would eat any. I WONDER WHY?

Called out at midnight and could hear the bobbins being dropped over the rail, as the deck crew were hauling the nets in. I pulled my boots on and smock and went into the messdeck. Had a quick cuppa and a rollie (cigarette) by the time my watch had gone on to the deck. The mate had been releasing the rollie, about 40 baskets. I stood by the winch when the Skipper sang out; 'Mate to the bridge.' Pemmy (Mate) passed me and said '250 off warp last time.' The cod ends were hanging over the side on the yoyo and the order came 'Let Go!' As they went over it pulled all the slack net with them and took the weight on the bobbins. We swung them over the side, quickly followed by the floatation (cans). The order came 'Lower the dhan lenos!' and when we had movement, we shot the doors away and the warps were payed away, with the messenger wire connected to the warp which picked up both wires and they were put into the towing block and we were back trawling again.

I was just walking aft when a few of the lads came running past me and I asked 'What's going on?' I was told someone had been fighting. I looked in the mess and Jerry had Terry B by the neck and had him lifted off the deck. I shouted Jerry and he turned and looked at me with stir crazy eyes. Something must have clicked, as he let go of him. This had been going on for a few days with Terry mouthing off. On reflection, I wonder what would have happened had I not gone into the mess. Terry went out the mess for his watch below. How do we keep them out of each other's way? The solution came very quickly.

The Skipper came down for a sarnie and said that we had to go in with a job on the pistons. We hauled the nets straight away and ran into Isa fjord with the local fitters standing by to work on the engines. We were alongside at 0700 hours and the agent came on board and spoke to the Skipper and by 0900 hours Terry B had packed his bag and was going off with the agent. We think that he had to pay for his own flight. The Skipper went into both messes and raised his voice asking if anyone else wanted to go and that he would have no trouble on his ship. We had no further trouble.

We were told to get our breakfast and that we would be sailing soon. Looked around the harbour and saw all the bright colours of the local houses, yellows, reds and blues. 1100 hours we let go and we were changing grounds as the Skipper has been told that the ice was moving towards land, so we were now going south. We just put a few lashings on the trawl as the trawl doors were dropped in prior to docking. To my surprise we had a rum issue and who was going to have Terry B's - you guessed right ME!

We had a lovely roast dinner of leg of lamb, mashed tatties, spring cabbage and fresh carrots, mint sauce with a thick gravy and plain duff which we could have with the main meal or dessert. I had it for both! Went on the bridge at 1230 hours and the Skipper told me to keep 6 miles off the north cape then head for Largeness. Skipper came back after lunch and called Jerry into his cabin after seeing him looking upset. Jerry came out alone after 5 or 6 minutes wiping his eyes and he took the ships wheel off me. He just said 'Thankyou' to me because if I had not shouted at him, he may now have been facing a murder charge!

Took the Deckie Learner on the bridge to get him used to steering the ship. The lads have made him a compass rose to teach him the points and during the cold and windy spells he has taken to fishing like a duck to water. Teatime soon approached and it was soon time for some well-earned shut eye. Not reading anymore gardening books! Instead reading Sven Hassle and Penal Regiments in Germany.

Does anyone want any mince pie - it's still not been eaten?

Called out at 0400 hours to haul the nets, had a bit of gash and now feeling less tired. We now have less than a week to go before we are docking. Only four days fishing left and looking forward to getting home. Net came on board with 20 baskets of fish, mostly codling. We are now fishing at Grimsey which is a small island off the east coast of Iceland. We put the net back over the side and went aft for a cuppa just before we went for the nightly rum ration. Eventually having our dram, the mate said; 'No fish next time.' And that we would be steaming again, this time to the Hoof and East Horns. No sooner had he spoken and we came fast. The net pulled loose of the obstruction and when we retrieved it, half of the belly was missing. So, we stuck a belly shooter into the net, ready for when the order came 'Drop in the doors' for a six-hour steam.

We finished cleaning the fish and breakfast was upon us. I was just walking aft when Snowy slipped and hurt his ankle whilst carrying a liver basket. Liver flew everywhere and the deck became like an ice rink. Most of the livers soon washed over the side. Jerry lifted Snowy up like a rag doll and took him aft. The Mate looked at the leg after breakfast and diagnosed a sprain and it soon bruised up. Snowy wanted to carry on which he did. Nearly two men down. One put ashore and another injured!

Really pleased with deckie learner and who was now on my watch.as nothing was too much for him. Always polite but clings to me like glue. Grabbed a couple of hours sleep after breakfast and lunch time soon came. On the menu was a pan of shackles, fresh busters with spotted dick duff for afters. Went on watch after lunch and as we were looking at the shoreline with snow-capped mountains. We saw movement in the water and it was a pod of Orcas (killer whales) going south and occasionally jumping out of the water.

Plenty of local pocket trawlers going about their business. Some waved at us and others ignored us. Just before tea was told to call the watches out and to change the bridles from the 50 fathoms and to put the 20 fathoms on. As instructed, pulled them off the winch and when the trawl went over, coiled the cables on to a cleat. I went onto the bridge to relieve the Skipper and sent a telegram home to the wife. Tea had been fish, chips and peas or cow pie with veggies which I opted for and then went below again, for a few hours rest.

Rolled out at midnight to shoot the trawl. The Northern Lights now lighting up the sky. People pay thousands to see this. We are now just putting the net over and the weather Is quite calm but turning colder. Hauled the net after 2 hours with 20 baskets of haddocks, a few plaice and a basket of large prawns. The haddocks were one of the best I've seen, very firm with large sizes. The net went over again and we hauled before breakfast. This time, as the net came up, it had nearly a full carcass of whalebone jaw that had been on the seabed a few years. Everyone started to boke and feel sick. One person started then a few more followed. When the bone came on board it was quickly returned to the sea. 30 baskets of fish had been in with this haul. I was told to put the board in the washer and give the fish a good wash. After finishing the fish, we used the winch steam hose to wash our wet gear and then just hosed down the decks. The smell lasted till nearly going home time.

Breakfast came and I had a nice fish sarnie with brown sauce and a cuppa. After breakfast, we cut the fifty fathom bridles down to thirties. Johnny Walker helped once more to take the turns out enabling the spike easy access. We completed the task just before hauling time. I was told to get a drink before we hauled. Twenty minutes later both trawl doors were hung on the dogs. The net soon came on board with the belly broken and thirty baskets of fish. We were told to lift the doors up out of the water, whilst we dodged south for an hour heading towards Kidney Bank.

We commenced mending the nets. Soon the fish had been cleaned and we also had a few more prawns. The whalebone smell was still very strong but the boking had now stopped. The Skipper told us to put the net over and looking around there must have been twenty / thirty ships in the area. The trawl had been put over the side without any incident. I then popped onto the bridge and I took the rum around. I gave Big Johnny Walker the gash dram for helping and I gave the deckie learner mine which he quickly gave back to me as he did not like the smell. I took the rum back onto the bridge and was told that this would be the last haul and as this was Monday, we were down for docking Thursday for Friday's fish market and to tell the mate to give him [the Skipper] a final tally of how much fish and what type we have to land.

I went down to the mess and told the cook the news and within 5 minutes it had gotten round that we were going home soon. The atmosphere changed to happiness very quickly. We hauled the nets at 1400 hours, with 40 baskets of mixed fish which was soon cleaned and put away down the fish room. We then started to put the deck boards and jockey boards away, secured the trawl and put the washer away. The fish room was then vacated and two baskets of mixed fish came up and was filleted. This was then put away in the fish room prior to docking. Everyone had about six pieces of fish and a couple of pounds of prawns each. Before we came off the deck, we payed away the old bridles that had been cut down. All hands went off the deck.

The Mate went on the bridge with the fish tally. Jerry and Eric, the Deckie Learner went on the bridge and I followed shortly after. The course was set for going home. We put the speed line over the stern and within twenty minutes the smell of soap and foo foo powder soon reached the bridge. Soon it would be our turn to do the same. The Mates tally had been 1,600 kits made up of 900 kits of cod, 400 kits haddocks, 200 kits coley, 100 mixed and 6 large halibuts. Watches had been set with my watch finishing at 1830 hours which came quickly. I was relieved by the mate. Steak pie for tea with mash, vegetables and onion gravy and fried fish, chips etc. followed by rhubarb crumble. Had my fill and then went for some shut eye. Immediately the channels start setting in.

Called out at 0245 hours for watch. Jerry and I are fully alert but Eric, the Deckie Learner asked if he could have an extra hour. We all went onto the bridge with a cuppa in our hands and relieved the deckies watch. Snowy is now in their watch and his ankle is now better. We are just passing the south end of the Faroes. The skies are zigzagging with the lights in the sky. When we are at home, we seldom see any stars but whilst at sea the skies are covered with them. Eric took the wheel first and when he has a spare moment, he keeps reading the compass Rose. Then I keep asking him to recite the opposites. Lovely lad who has not had a good start in life but he has never cheeked anybody, unlike me.

Quite a lot of boats are in the area, in close proximity. We are not far from a fishing bank. I do hope that the Skipper doesn't get out and see what they are catching. Can't tell you and it is not just me but we are all so tired. We are working eighteen hours and having only six hours sleep. We are very fortunate as before I started fishing there was no watch below.

I went on the boat deck at 0400 hours and read the trail log and we are doing 11.4 knots on average. We have now altered course to pass Dennis Head which is a landmark on the Papa Westray. We should be there by teatime-ish. The tide and a northerly 4 are keeping us steady with a gentle roll every so often. Eric is fascinated by the shooting stars and Jerry has popped down to make a pot of spesh tea but he is using the one that I opened already. He his saving his to take home for Rose.

The other day I had to write a statement about Jerry and Terry B regarding him going home last week and the incident that happened. We all know that Jerry has poor literacy so Eric wrote down his statement for him, as he told him what had happened. Jerry then signed the statement. A fresh cuppa came up and Jerry had cleaned the messes. At 0500 hours the smell of fresh bread reached us. I filled the log book and radio logs at 0700 hours as the watch and daymen were being called. The sun was shining and it seemed to be getting warmer. I handed over the watch to the Mate. Fresh busters thickly spread with echo margarine, filled with spam fritter and egg which was dribbling down the sides and running down my hands, delicious. After eating, we had a quick smoke and spoke with the daymen. I asked to be called for lunch, if they didn't see me before then. Sleep approached and so did the channels.

During the afternoon I went on the deck with the daymen. They were overhauling the trawl whist I cleaned out the cod ends and gave them the once over. 1500 hours we had a quick cuppa and then back on the deck to finish off our tasks. We lashed the trawl up and gave her a quick wash down with the donkey hose. All cabin and bridge mats had been taken out during the morning and now they were all taken back to their cabins etc. Teatime came which was a mixed grill being the main meal with fish on the menu, as well. Cornflake tart for afters with a thick custard. Relieved the watch at 1830 hours and we have just passed Duncansby Head. Jerry was on the wheel and I went in to the chart room to set a course three miles off Rattary Head.

It seemed like only yesterday that we had passed this place. During the watch we ran into a few small pocket trawlers plying their trade, with supply boats travelling up to Lerwick and the oil rigs. As the sun began to set, we could see the loom of the land in the distance. The Skippers asked the Deckie Learner if he wanted to clean his cabin and if he did his bond would be paid for his chores. Travelling along the coast car headlights could be seen as they travelled up and down the coastline. Tonight, there is a full moon and you can see the glow of the phosphorus being churned up on our stern. Eric had now finished the cleaning and was back on the ships wheel. The watch was called out and we handed over to the Mate. We all went aft. Sleep soon befell us all.

Wednesday, we hugged the coastline and the weather remained calm. Excellent visibility with calm seas. We passed Flamborough Head just after midnight. At 0500 hours we dropped the anchor which the crew had cut for cards and after breakfast they would go ashore on the tug party. The Mate had the watch on the bridge I woke up and had some breakfast and finished packing my gear. At 0900 hours the Brenda Fisher came alongside us and took eight of our crew off and into the royal dock basin where they had to climb the steps up to get to the quay, cross the lock gates onto fish dock road and then to riby square. They all had to go in different directions. I went up to the galley and was just about to make a drink when I was called up to the bridge.

The Skipper took me to his cabin and then my world shattered. He Told me that I wouldn't be coming back next trip. 'I'M SACKING YOU!' I was gutted. I asked him why and he said that when I joined last trip, he knew that I had a lot to learn but this trip and parts of last trip he felt that I had proved to him that I am now capable of going in any ship and could do the BOSUNS/THIRDHANDS JOB. He said that he had no hesitation in recommending me. So, from feeling upset I could see now his reasoning. He was telling me that I could stand on my own two feet. We shook hands and he said, 'No hard feelings.' My reply was; 'I understand!'

1600hrs the Brenda Fisher took us into the dock and we tied up alongside the fish dock berth. I was told to leave the wheel amidships and then I could go. The Skipper passed me a bottle of whisky and said that we would see each other later. We had tied up at No. 1 berth with only two deep water vessels and one westerly boat. There were three North Sea ships landing with about 4.500 kits in total. The wife came into meet me and the father-in-law stayed to see to the Customs Officers.

I went below and saw the rest of the crew. I told them that I had been sacked but didn't go into detail. Most of the lads shook my hand and I said my farewells. I went on the quayside and got into our car. On the way home I told the wife; 'Your dad has just sacked me but I understood why.' When I got home, I had along soak in the bath but not before I gave some fish to our next-door neighbour and another neighbour across the road. At 1800 hour I took a fry of fish to Dave's chippy on the corner of our Street to have it fried.

The next day [Landing Day] I went down to Billy Raymond's had my haircut and told him I would pay him later in the day. I walked home from there and had a quick soak in the bath again. I borrowed a fiver off our Edie who was our neighbour and Cheryl's auntie. About 1100 hours I took a slow walk to the Clee Park and walked into the front room and ordered a lager from the barmaid. Harold Brennan was sat around a table with his family. The first drink went down like milk and so I ordered another pint but drank this one slowly. I went outside to the taxi rank to go down dock and arrived at the office. When I went inside both Bill Batty and Charlie Ward asked; 'What's gone on?' I said; 'What with Terry B?' 'No' they said 'you getting the sack'. I told them that it was ok and left it like that. They said that we landed 1,750 kits and made £26,500. I was well impressed with that.

I had a couple of hours to kill before I had arranged to meet Cheryl, who was working. I left the office with my settlings and went for my fry of fish when I saw Fred Dickinson who was Boston's Ships Runner. He told me to go to see him next Wednesday as he might have a ship for me. I had a quick pint in the Humber Wicket and the usual faces were in there. I had another half in the Albion but first I paid Billy Raymond for my haircut. 1300 hours met the wife in the White Knight and had a pint and then on to the bank to put the settlings in. The wife took a sandwich back to work and I had a couple of pints in the Corporation Arms where there was always a good atmosphere and I knew quite a few of the patrons. I had to go back to Billy Raymond's to pick my fish up and walked to the Clee Park. I had a quick pint in the bar and then went home to have a nap before Cheryl came home. I gave our Edie her fiver back with another fry. Now I was back home I changed into some leisure gear and had a nap on the couch.

One week later I signed on as THIRD HAND on the BELGAUM

10

Belgaum

Going Down Dock On Friday
To Sign On The Belgaum

The Crew:

TOMMY WHITCOMBE SKIPPER
IZZY WOODS RELIEF MATE
RON TELFORD BOSUN
with **BOBBY ELLIOT,**
THOMSPON,
HARRY SCOTTER,
JOHNNY CHASE,
JOHN SUMPTER,
NORMAN SCOTT
and **GORDON,**
Derek Bartholomew,
Spider,
Lamley,
Turkey Taylor,
Sid the Chief,
Harry Chard 2nd,
Alec Webster - Cook,
Young Billy Esky - Galley Boy,
Ron Davison - Liver Man

The wife took me down dock today. Firstly, I went to the cashiers and gave my P45 to Frank and he told me that I had a tax rebate to come. I ended up with £30. I collected the money and was about to go down stairs when Fred Parkes opened the door. I had a few minutes chat with him and he said: 'Well done' to me on obtaining my third hands certificate. In due course I went down the stairs and into the ships runner's office and signed on the Belgaum as Third Hand [Bosun]. I went back upstairs to obtain a £5 sub.

Cheryl then took me to the North Wall to look for the ship which we soon found. In the back of the car, I had my bedding and sea gear which I took on board. I shouted to the watchman who quickly appeared and shouted; 'Who's there!' I answered him and told him who I was and he helped me put my gear into my berth. I told him that I would see him on Friday morning. I climbed off the ship, got into the car and drove off the docks. Whilst driving I asked the wife if we should go out tonight. 'Yes' was the reply. I never went out the night before we sailed as I was always in a mood on the day we went to sea.

The day before sailing I was not always in the best of moods. It's all down to being away from loved ones. Going visiting to say goodbye to loved ones within the family was not always easy for me. My father-in-law, Bill Ferrand, gave me confidence and encouragement when he told me that I could go in any ship and do the Bosuns work. I spent the last night with my wife and son and felt very apprehensive about sailing tomorrow. We are ordered for 0700 hours so it's an early night for us all.

Very restless and although trying to sleep, I can only catnap. I got up at 0600 hours and have several cuppas and a dozen fags. 0705 hours I keep looking out the window for the taxi. I take a quick nogging of rum to try to settle my nerves, 0715 hours the taxi arrives and Vic, the driver, knocks on the door. I give him my bag then go upstairs to kiss my wife and son goodbye. Just wished that we had another day in dock. Cheryl used to say that I was always miserable but when she heard me greetings everyone in the taxi it was as thought I was going on holiday. No one knew how I was feeling because spirits needed to be high. In reality no one wanted to go but it was our livelihood and we really had no choice.

A quick ride to the North Wall, dropped off at the ship, climbed the steep ladder with my gear over my shoulder, climbed over the whaleback and aft to the crews' quarters. I was spotted by the crew who I knew from sailing in her previously. Their words; 'What are you doing here?' My reply; 'I'm the thirdhand now.' A couple of them laughed, until I put my gear into my cabin. I went ashore to Coleridge's (outfitter) and then back on board the ship. Alec the cook spotted me saying that he had heard that I was Bosun. He then said; 'Good for you and don't let the crew bully you.' The person who had been acting Bosun [without a ticket] stated that if I needed a hand he would help (Turkey Taylor) which was nice of him. I heard on the tannoid 'Bosun to the bridge'. I climbed onto the bridge and there stood the Skipper in his grey jumper with a muffler around his neck with a pair of old clumpers on. He then shook my hand saying; 'Welcome aboard again,' The time now was 1000 hours. I then stood behind the helm obeying various orders. We slipped out of the dock and into the river Humber.

We had gone around the lightship when the mate came up and took over the watch. He told me who my watchmates were and I then vacated the bridge. I proceeded aft for something to eat and enjoyed bacon, eggs and sausages, that went down nicely. I sat down in the officer's mess and introduced myself to the Radio Operator, a young kid from Scotland and he seemed very friendly. The Chief was sitting in there as well and he was always gasping for breath. I left and made my way to my cabin. I changed my gear and fell asleep for a couple of hours. I was called out for 'watcho', with Ron Davidson and Derek Bartholomew. It was nice being on watch without having to steer the ship by hand. When we get this first day over, we will settle down again.

2300 hours and off watch. Just time for a quick sarnie and then lights out.

Called out for breakfast. We had a full English with Lincolnshire sausages, back bacon, beans with fresh fried tomatoes, complete with fresh busters and daddies' sauce. What a way to start the day. I went on the bridge and relieved the Mate (Izzy Woods). We were just passing Aberdeen and we could see the harbour three miles in the distance. Ships from here don't usually sail until about 1100 hours which I believe is some kind of port ruling. However, unlike Grimsby, ships can sail in and out of the harbour all day, whilst Grimsby is controlled by lock gates and the tides. The Skipper rolled out and sent one of my watchmates to make him a cup of tea whilst relieving me so I could go on the deck. I put on my boots, smock, hat and muffler (scarf) and proceeded on to the deck. Turkey Taylor took me around the deck fore hold etc. explaining where things were and stated that we had three pairs of cod ends, two of which were brand new and the one on the spare trawl had been end to ended. This has given me a good start.

The weather is a southerly 3 with clear visibility. We lowered the yoyo davit, erected the washer and started to put up the fish pound boards. We popped aft for a mid-morning cuppa. We were back on the deck just after 1000 hours erecting the rest of the boards and jockey boards. I sharpened my knife on the whiffling stick, and tested it on a piece of rope for sharpness. Satisfied with the sharpness I had a look down the fore hold and whaleback to familiarise myself with the layout again. 1100 hours the bond was being dished out. I went aft to my cabin and took my deck gear off, picked up a pillow case and proceeded to the wheelhouse. We were just approaching Rattary Point which

I duly logged, distance and bearing and set a course to pass Duncansby Head at a distance of three miles.

The Radio Operator and Ron, my watchmate, had been filling empty vinegar and cordial bottles with rum from glass jars, protected by basket ware. The rule of thumb, I believe, was that one litre of rum was taken out of the jar which was replaced with one litre of water. I am not too sure whether this is the correct amount as fifty years have passed. My watchmates and I were the last to receive the bond which consisted of tobacco, cigarettes, fag papers, Typhoo tea, Libby's milk, assorted nuts in dark chocolate, large tins of Quality Street. I was given a case of Long-Life beer whilst the ratings were given 12 cans each. Lunch time arrived and, on the menu, we had Onion duff, roast beef, mashed tatties, carrots and cabbage, with homemade oxtail soup to start. After lunch I went for a nap whist the dayman and the mate sorted out the fish room.

Called out for tea which was cow pie, chips, peas with baked rice pudding for afters. I had my tea 2nd sitting with the Operator and the Chief. We began having a chin wag about our families and where we lived etc. I looked outside, through the porthole and we were all battened down as we were now in the Pentland Firth which is a very dangerous place to be. Five different tides meet in one place which cause whirlpools as they meet together. Many a ship has foundered here but with the tide right you can soon pass through but, going against the tide, it seems to take ages. On looking out of the porthole we are travelling through quickly with the Old Man of Hoy standing proudly by itself. Soon passing Dunnet Head and now heading towards the Faroe Islands.

I could hear music and laughter coming from the focsal. The crew spotted me and asked if I wanted a can of Red

Bass which I declined but said perhaps another time. I lay down and started reading Sven Hassle Blitzkrieg which are the type of books you can't put down. It was soon watcho so I went and had a quick rinse and brushed my teeth. I could still hear the lads having a good time. I went back to my cabin, collected six cans of beer and gave it to the crew in the party berth. I climbed the steps to the bridge and took over the watch. There was a full moon reflecting on the water, not a cloud in sight, with thousands of stars twinkling through the night with the occasional shooting star.

The Skipper had been rolled in a couple of hours when we heard the sirens going in the engine room. The Skipper rolled out and told to me to go see what's up down there. I was just about to go when the engineer popped up to the bridge saying that they had a leaking liner, they have eased down the speed and that they would let us know what was happening. The Skipper said; 'Where are we now?' and showed him on the chart. We have now altered course for Lerwick which is 40 miles away. We expected to arrive after breakfast with the fitters awaiting on the quayside.

Went below at 0300 hours heading towards Lerwick. Awoke to the sounds of the engines going astern. I went on the deck with the crew who had just finished tying the ship alongside the quay. We were at the ferry terminal with the Lerwick Hotel close by. The shoreside fitters came aboard with spares for the engine room and specialist tools. I went inside for a smoke and a cuppa. Some of the crews were eager to go ashore and one by one they went on the bridge to ask permission to go ashore which was granted. They were told to come back to the ship by 1500 hours. Only a couple of the lads came back and by 1700 hours the rest followed, all the merrier from their time ashore.

Just after tea the engines were restarted with things seeming to be ok. We heard that we would be sailing at 1900 hours. When the fitters left the ship and threw our mooring ropes off, we cleared Lerwick by 2000 hours. We were now heading on a northerly course towards the Faroe Islands and then onwards towards Iceland. The weather had begun to freshen and the ship started a gentle roll now and again. Behind us we could see the loom of the land, with a few fishing boats trying to earn a living around the Western Isles. This was a favourite area for the 'Cat' boats.

I came off watch at 2300 hours when we were just passing Esha Ness and approaching Sullom Voe from a distance. I popped in the mess for quick bite of something to eat and then crashed into my bunk. I was called out for breakfast but it seemed that I had just closed my eyes and watcho had been called. I had a boiled egg, a round of toast with a bacon buster. I took over the watch and at 0830 hours went on the deck with the daymen. Most of the crew were complaining of hangovers and all agreeing that they would not be drinking anymore. We released the trawl from its lashing, took the chains off and gave the trawl a quick once over.

We were just passing the south end of the Faroes and was called to the bridge to dish the rum out. I walked through the engine room shouting; 'Rum oh!' Both engineers spotted me and came to the aft alleyway were they both had their dram. The cook and daymen soon followed. Took the rum on to the bridge and gave my watchmates their ration. The daymen asked if I would give them a sub from my beer issue and I passed four cans to them. I had a can then went to the bridge. My watch called the next watch out.

After dinner went on the deck to overhaul the net, when the mate said that he didn't need me so I went and rolled in. I woke up startled and I could hear the banging on the deck as the bobbins were being lifted. The time was about 1700 hours. I looked out onto the deck as the trawl went over and saw Turkey at the after end of the trawl deck. He shouted to me that I was not needed on the deck with my watchmates so I went for a cup of spesh. All square shouted and the lads come in as tea time was fast approaching. I sat down to tea and the Skipper asked if I have settled in and that we were now at the Whaleback fishing ground. A few ships had been catching plenty of cod. I finished my tea and watches had been set. We were now on fishing watches.

Called out 0130 hours for hauling time. Whilst my watch had been below, on the last haul we had 50 kits of cod and ling. This is going to be my first time hauling on here. I heard the release of the towing block as I put on my wet gear. The weather is quite fresh, blowing Northerly 6. I walked on the deck to a face full of spray which soon woke me up. I took my place near the winch and counted the marks on the warp as it came in. We had 400 fathoms aft when we started hauling and now, we are down to are last 100. Two more marks came in and I shouted 'LAST FIFTY'. The Mate told me to hold the 'SHORTMARK' which I did until told to start hauling. The after door came up first, then the fore door, both linkages were unlocked, with the dhan lenos now in both bollards, bobbins came in followed by the floats. I handed the winch over to Bart whilst I commanded the deck duties. We heaved on the lazy deckie, then trapping the nets, using small beckets and links, we started bringing the cod ends closer to the ship's sides. Two or three lifts later we put the halving becket on and lifted the cod ends aboard. Another productive haul of about 60 baskets which was mostly large cod. Retied the cod line and put the net back into the water.

As I made my way to the ships rail the ship dipped her rail. The starboard side filled with heavy water which soon cleared through the duckpond. My boots were full of water and as I walked all I could hear was 'squelch, squelch'. My toes were now beginning to feel warm. I took my boots off on the winch grating and discovered they were half full with water. I was told to lower the dhan lenos and the cod line doors, shortly after paying the warps away, I shouted; 'last fifty'. The ship then eased in. The messenger hook was put onto the forward warp and I shouted; 'Let go'. We then heaved on the messenger wire which in turn pulled both warps into the towing block which was then closed and secured by a large pin. We reversed the wire and a voice from aft shouted; 'ALL SQUARE AFT'. I went off the deck to change my boots and socks putting the wet ones in the engine room gratings to dry. My watch popped onto the bridge for our night-time rum issue and I lit a cigarette. I used the galley whiffling stick to sharpen my knife and proceeded back on the deck to take up my position in the after-fish pounds, cleaning the fish whilst listening to country music. 'OH, THE JOYS OF BEING A FISHERMAN!'

During the last haul Archie, the fore door man, trapped his hand in the dog chain whilst hauling. We pulled the rest of the trawl in and proceeded to take him in to Sedysford which is just outside the pilot launch. We took Archie off and he was taken to the local hospital. He had three broken fingers and he was flown home a couple of days later. Two hours after dropping Archie off we were back fishing at a ground called East of the Horns. On the first tow we caught 40 baskets of prime haddocks with a few large prawns which we ate over the next few days. The next haul we had a small hole in the belly of the net which we just laced in and put the net back over the side.

The weather began to scream and the Skipper shouted down to the deck to get the gear aboard and drop the gear inboard. A heavy spray which stung the eyes was now coming over the ship's sides. The wind was coming from the direction of the North East with a light frost which is now beginning to cling to the metalwork. The net was now onboard, the trawl doors were dropped in, with a few lashings put on the trawl with the use of both the fore and after Gilson's, the net had been secured. We picked up our gutting knifes and cleaned the 40 baskets cod and haddock. It took us just over an hour to clean and put the fish away. We secured the cod line to the forward bollard and opened the scupper doors for the seas to run away whilst dodging on location. I stood by the fish room hatch and shouted down; 'Have you nearly finished down there?' when a large wave came over the side and knocked me off my feet and took my breath away. I had not been the only one. Bart had been pushed alongside of the fish washer and grazed his forehead which was weeping slightly with blood. The fish room men came out and onto the main deck and all four of us made our way slowly aft. The liver door and all main doors were now battened down.

I went to my cabin and put on a change of clothes. I dropped all my wet gear into the sit in bath and ran some hot water adding some OMO wash powder. I was just about to pour a cuppa when I was summoned to the bridge to dish out the morning rum. The Skipper is in a good mood and says that some ships are still fishing in this weather but wouldn't until the weather abates. On the last haul we caught a medium sized halibut and it would be on the lunchtime menu. I took the rum around which had not been an easy task as the ship was 'rocking and rolling'. I. decided that it would be easier to sit down in the mess to dish out the ration and when I had finished, I returned the rum back to the bridge. The weather had now increased to a force 9 from the North and it was snowing heavily and clinging to the bridge windows. The sea spray would wash off the snow from the windows as we dodged. The deckies watch were sent to the bridge with Terry in charge.

Lunchtime came which was either a big pan of shackles or halibut soup. I went for the latter which turned out to be a good choice, as I enjoyed it. I took over the watch and we were heading towards Vopna to get a lee off the land. A few other ships have had the same idea but we were all spread out from each other. The weather started to ease as we closed in towards the land. We were 3 miles off Vopna and just before tea we dropped the anchor. Tea time came and watch below followed. What a day - I think I will send some flowers home tomorrow.

Called out at breakfast time and had a nice piece of haddock with a fresh buster. I applied some butter and could feel it running on my chin as I were eating it. I put on my wet gear and with a couple of lads helping me on the whaleback, we heaved the anchor up. One man went down the chain locker to flake the anchor chain as it came up. Only three lengths of cable and the anchor was secured. We put a few rags around the hawser pipe and applied cement as a sealant. Soon we were heading out of the shelter of the land and into the open sea towards the fishing grounds.

I could not belief that the wind had gone but we still had a large rolling swell. With a good forecast we steamed on and after 2 hours we were putting the trawl back over the side and hopefully back to earning a living. The time was now 1030 hours. I popped on to the bridge to dish out the rum issue and took it back onto the bridge when finished. I then went back to my cabin for a can of beer before lunch. I relieved the skipper whilst he had something to eat and when he returned, I went for mine. On the menu was corn beef fritters, chips, eggs and beans or halibut soup. I had a cup full of soup followed by the fry up, I had just about finished my dinner when the warps started to pull out and we became fast on the seabed.

The net came fast on the sea bed and we were told to knock out the wires in the towing block. We started to heave on the wires but we are stuck solid. The ship came hard to starboard, when suddenly we were released from the fastener on the seabed. The trawl doors came up full of mud followed by the dhan lenos. The headline had parted with little damage to the net with about 40 baskets of fish. We replaced the headline and shot the net away again.

I looked around and saw that there were with plenty of boats around us. The nearest being the St. Dominic with its large funnel, the Boston Concord with its streamline build and we had just about finished on the deck when we passed the Northern Queen. I waved at the father-in-law. I liked sailing with him, he gave me my start, now I'm on my own and I just want to get on with things. Twelve hours ago, we were in a force 9 but now the winds have eased down. The visibility is about twenty miles plus. We hauled again just prior to teatime with 100 baskets of large cod. After the fish had been gutted, I went down the fish room to have a sneaky look around and I guess about 700 kits. Not bad for 5 days' work. The Skipper went for his tea and when he returned to the bridge, I went down for mine. On the menu we had pork chops, mashed potato, carrots, green beans with mint sauce, with treacle duff for afters. Half way through my afters and we came fast again but this time I was going to bed. I finished my tea, went below and within minutes I had fallen asleep.

Called out at midnight with 50 baskets of fish and told they were just putting the net back over. I got dressed, popped into the mess for a quick cuppa and a smoke. The gear was now over the side and the Mate came aft and said that they had changed the net at teatime. We started to repair the broken one and all it needed now was a new top and lower wing. I went into the fish pounds and started gutting the fish. Listening to Marty Robbins singing 'Deep in the West Texas town of Ell Paso'. Just what I needed, first thing after rolling out. Then Patsy Clyne singing 'CRAZY' came on and I was just thinking, 'We must be 'CRAZY' doing this work. Working 18 hours a day, appalling conditions, sleep deprived, cold, wet and generally feeling sorry for myself. However, these feeling soon passed once the fish was gutted and the decks were washed down. My watch popped onto the bridge for our evening dram of rum.

The Mate told us we would be hauling at 0500 hours which gave us a couple of hours to finish the net. We completed the repair and stored it in a net bin over the after gallows. We hauled and shot the net away just before breakfast. Only 10 baskets of crap this haul and had a quick look in the cod ends using the yoyo and the Gilson - all was good. Settled down for breakfast which was porridge, spam fritters and bacon with fresh busters. After eating I managed to grab an hour before hauling time, in fact it was 3 hours.

When we hauled at 1000 hours, we had the distinct smell of a rotting carcass. The Skipper shouted to me; 'Have you got trapped wind?' As we began pulling the net in you could hear some of the lads making horrible gagging sounds and being sick. It is impossible to describe the smell of rotting carcasses but this time it had been a dead porpoise. The meat was squelching with the tightening of the net and everyone was either puking and retching. There had been little or no fish in the cod ends so the Skipper told us to undo the cod ends and lower it over the side which we did. Unfortunately, before the exercise was complete, some rotting meat fell in the fish pounds. I was told to tie the cod ends and shoot away again. 'ALL SQARE AFT.' Then straight into the fish pounds to try to wash away the smell of decaying meat off the deck. I took my gear off and went into the bathroom and had a good scrub with lifebuoy soap to try and lose that horrible smell.

After several days fishing at the Telegraph Hoof and Horns, we finished fishing at the Workingman's Bank. We are now 16 days away, when suddenly from the bridge window the Skipper says; 'Two more hauls and we are going Home!' Immediately we all shouted 'HOORAY'. We had 1,400 kits of mostly prime fish and we will be in for the weekend. We hauled just after breakfast with the belly ripped. The Skipper shouts; 'Lace it nets up!' which we did and put the net back over. At 1100 hours we hauled, about 40 baskets of mixed fish. The order came; 'Drop those doors in, we are going HOME!'

Smiles and laughter were now on every face. The doors are now in with a couple of lashings on the trawl. I called on the bridge to pick up the poison (rum) which I dished out. I then went into the fish room until lunch time. On today's menu we had cow pie with all the trimmings. We finished our lunch then back gutting the fish and by 1330 hours all the fish was cleaned and put away. All the pound boards were given a good wash before being taken down a put away. Next the washer was taken down and we washed the gutting area and around the fish room hatch. The guiding-on gear was tied down next and placed behind the winch, putting lashings through the wheels. The tasks completed we went off the deck together. I took my wets off and went on to the bridge to take over from the Skipper. Teatime came and, on the menu, we had ham, eggs and chips or fried fish, followed by Manchester tart for afters. I filled my boots, so to speak. I went below to have 8 hours sleep as I am on watch again at 0300 hours. Ten days of doing 18 hours a day makes you physically drained and in just over a couple of days' times we will all be back at home with our loved ones.

We passed the Faroe Islands two days ago. The Northern Lights had been amazing this voyage but we just take it for granted. The weather has been kind to us and with not much mending of the nets. We only changed the trawl once as there were only minor tears, here and there which had made it a fairly easy voyage. We spent a few hours on the deck undoing the laced net and repairing it properly. The decks were scrubbed, with most of the interior cleaned. Just a bit of brasso needed to be applied here and there.

The Scottish coast had looked amazing as we sailed passed. We were able to see quite a few small fishing vessels going about their trade. We were now passing Scarborough with its Castle in the background and just in the distance Flamborough Head with its lighthouse standing proud on the cliffs. Three hours later I was called to the bridge and told to take the helm in, hand steering as we navigated the rivers buoyage system. As we approached the Burcom, the tug, Alfred Bannister, came to take our ropes and we were taken into the fish docks, berth no 3, as there were a couple more deep-water boats plus westerly and North Sea vessels. We have been told that the fish prices are good but let's wait and see tomorrow. I was walking off the boat when I spotted Cheryl. I gave her a hug and then got into the car for our journey home. The first thing Cheryl asked me was; 'When are you sailing again?' She wanted to know how long she had to be my sea gear washed and dried ready for the next trip.

After a good night's sleep, waking up naturally, instead of being called out for work, to hold and play with your baby son is what put a smile on my face. Just thinking about it makes me smile, even today. A full English breakfast with all the trimmings and a long soak in the bath. My suit, dry cleaned whilst I was away, was laid on the bed with a clean shirt and tie. All dressed to go down dock I went downstairs had a coffee, kissed the wife and son. I made arrangements to meet the wife at lunchtime and left the house and headed towards the Clee Park. I just had a pint in there and noticed the regulars were already discussing today's news. As the weather was nice, I walked down dock, firstly calling in to Arthur Lacey's to get my fry of fish. I then across the road to see Fred, the Ships Runner at Boston's, who told me that I had a good report and we have made £26,000.

Not bad for 19 days at sea from Iceland. I had a quick pint in the Humber but didn't see anybody I knew. I popped into Billy Raymond's and had my haircut. From there over to the bank to put my settlings in. I just kept a bit aside as I would be meeting the wife after lunch to go shopping, but first we were going into the Pea Bung to have a nice lunch of fish and chips.

11

Belgaum – Norway Coast

Enjoyed my 60 hours in dock, but it's getting harder leaving my wife and son at home. Every time I'm at Home it feels like I am on my honeymoon. The taxi driver knocked on the door at 0800 hours and this time it's Ron doing the pickups. I'm the last to be picked up and its straight on to the docks. As we are going down Cleethorpes Road, we are passing shift workers going to and from their places of work. It's now the first week in April and people are walking around in shirt sleeves We arrived onto the north wall and I climbed the ladder onto the whaleback. I ventured aft, chucked my bag in the cabin and then visited the outfitters. I went into Coleridge's buying gloves and magazines plus a tin of Fray Bentos, as my emergency rations. I went into Vincent's with one of our crew and that slimy man asked whether I wanted anything. My reply was; 'Piss off - I will never buy from you again as you've tried to rob me on numerous occasions.' I left the store and went back to the ship. I had a quick cuppa and was then called to the bridge for sailing.

The Skipper tells us that Izzy, the Mate, will not sailing this trip as he has gone to the hospital with a suspected broken jaw and that he shouldn't mess about with other people's wives. The Brenda Fisher assisted us out of the dock and off we go on our new venture. My watchmate, who was the liver man last trip, kept a low profile and a new crewmate, Jerry P, who asked to come on my watch. I'm not going to argue with him. Rounded the Lightship. Johnny Stevens, the Mate, relieved me and the course is set for NNE.

Came off watch, unpacked my bag and put all my work gear to hand. A couple of the lads asked if I wanted a tinny which I refused or a dram but again I said no thanks you. I popped in the messdeck, had a bite to eat and then rolled in until teatime. I didn't get much sleep as the party berth had been in full swing and after every can the volume became louder. I was called for tea and afterwards I went on watch with my watchmates who were Jerry P. and Johnny C. One hour into our watch we approached about a hundred small Russian fishing boats who were either catching sprats or herring.

The Skipper told me not to alter course for them and that they would alter for me which they did. To the East of us we could see plenty of lights and flames as we pass the Ekofisk oil field. The weather at this time was a light southerly breeze, with visibility 12 miles plus. There were plenty of vessels going about their daily business. My watchmates and I were chatting idly about our time ashore and what we did in our short time at home. This was the first time that our Skipper has been to Norway and we were all up for the challenge. Jerry made a pot of special from last trips bond which I had kept aside for this trip. Plenty of platforms are beginning to appear on the horizon with a few fishing boats going about their trade. 1045 hours our relief watch was called and by 2300 hours we had handed over. I went straight off the bridge, ventured to my cabin and rolled in for the night.

Called out at breakfast with the smell of kippers in the air. Headed straight into the mess and filled my plate. A dream come true, with the fresh busters and butter running down my chin. The watch came down and told me that the Skipper would be taking my watch. When breakfast was finished, I went into my cabin and put on my boots and smock. I went into the messdeck and discussed what we would be doing and went on the deck at 0800 hours. We lowered the yoyo (used to take the cod ends out), lowered the fish washer and started to put the iron gratings and deck boards up (used for containing the fish). Just ahead of us was a mighty oil drilling platform standing proudly on the horizon, surrounded by big orange floats, which were attached to anchors and Maersk supply boats with their distinctive light blue hulls. We left the trawl tied up as it was overhauled and repaired going home last trip.

One or two of the lads kept being sick, too much booze from yesterday's party I suspect! Almost ten hours so time to go aft for a quick smoke and a cuppa. I popped into my cabin and came out with four cans in my hand and gave them to the lads for a livener. I was called the best Bosun in Grimsby but maybe I will be called a different name tomorrow!

We had lots of old net under the whaleback and I told the lads to drag it all out and that I will sort it with the deckie learner. I started cutting pieces up 100 mesh by 50 mesh, 50 by 50, etc. and put them in the net bin in case we needed them later. The markings were done with twine knots and the lads were making spare wings, headline floats attached, with a couple making new belly and baiting's.

Everything was going along nicely when the Fire Alarm activated. We all went to our MUSTER STATIONS and the Mate did a headcount and confirmed no one missing. He then told us that this was a drill. He reminded the crew what they should do in an emergency, i.e., warm clothing, water, flares etc. All crew were then stood down and we were told that the bond was open but we would be only getting a three-day quota until we reach the fishing grounds.

Just a few feet from us dolphins were gliding through the water whilst the seagulls flew effortlessly by the ship's sides.

I was one of the last to get the bond and was given, 1 tin tobacco, 200 Benson & Hedges, 6 packets of papers, with a case of red devils and a nogging of rum. I took them down to my cabin and by this time it was lunchtime. After lunch I went back on to the bridge and filled in the log books and waited for the Mate. I looked into the radar and noticed lots of large echoes which turned out to be oil rigs. I handed over the watch and asked the Mate if he needed me. John's reply was 'Nah, I'll be with them.' The menu for dinner was, onion duff, roast tatties, carrots, beans with roast lamb. The cook gave me the muscle part of the leg and the bone to eat. I felt as though I needed rolling down the stairs to my cabin. I slipped my gear off and rolled into my bunk, with the gardening magazines from last trip. A couple of this trips were laid on my seat locker. It looks like I'm converting the lads to gardeners.

After a couple of days steaming, we had passed many a landmark with plenty of shipping. The night skies were amazing to watch, so mesmerising with the Northern lights flickering through the sky. We are now among the Lofton Islands and nearing Lodigen pilot station. It only seems like yesterday when I had been here in the Northern Queen. High in the mountains an Aldiss light began sending morse code and asking for our ships name and number. The Skipper told me to answer him on our equipment, seeing as I had only recently left college. I flashed them our name – 'Bravo, Echo. Lima. Golf. Alpha. Uniform. Mike' BELGAUM. All was acknowledged and then on channel 14 we were called by the pilots. The Skipper answered and again they asked the name. The Skipper replied. Banana,

Egg, Lemon, Grape, Apple, Ugly-fruit, Melon. They all laughed and so did we.

The Pilot boat came alongside without KBS as a pilot but we had two different ones who seemed very friendly and polite. Fresh milk and venison came on board to have over the coming days. Courses were set and we settled down to steer various courses through the fjords. We could see homes lit up in the mountains plus headlights of traffic going about their business. The Mate came up to relieve me and at the appointed hour my watch vacated the wheelhouse.

1700 hours called out and told to get the ropes ready for tying up as we would be going alongside in Tromso with an engine room job. I quickly dressed and went straight into the mess for a quick cuppa and a smoke. After about ten minutes the watch came down and said that we would be tying up starboard side. We went on to the Tromso deck slipping and sliding as water and soot was everywhere as it was spewing out of the funnel. I have heard of this before and it was down to a leaky liner in the cylinder head. I climbed onto the whaleback and helped pulling the ropes up and getting them ready to tie up. About fifteen minutes later all ropes were secured. We sprinkled plenty of sand on the deck just to prevent anyone falling in the oily conditions. I had just taken my gear off, when the engineers opened the engine room door and all four of the engineers came out lathered in soot etc. They had a few moments on the deck getting some fresh air telling us that we had cracked cylinder heads and that they needed changing. We carried a couple of spares and we were now awaiting local fitters to carry out the repairs. We were told that we would be in dock for at least twenty-four hours.

Teatime was approaching so time for a quick wash of hands and into the crew's mess and had my tea. There was no room in the mess I usually ate in as the Skipper, Mate, two Engineers plus two Pilots and a Radio Officer were already seated. I tucked into a cooked meal of venison, mash, cabbage, turnip and swede followed by a chocolate duff and chocolate sauce for afters. I had my tea and went on to the bridge to keep an eye on the ropes.

The Customs and Agent came on board doing their businesses. A couple of local lads appeared in a car with chains on their wheels asking if we had any beer to sell. When they saw the Custom Officer leaving, they scarpered. At about 1900 hours a couple of lads were going ashore to stretch their legs. I spotted the Galley Boy and Deckie Learner going ashore and told them to keep together and enjoy themselves. Little did I know that they would find the Monopole, Off-Licence and purchased a bottle of ADV Ankit which they drank on the quayside. After about an hour and a half I could hear them from a distance singing as they headed back to the ship. I saw them aboard and later popped down below just to make sure they were ok. They were fine and were just talking rubbish like most drunken people, so I left them to it.

Shoreside fitters arrived about 2100 hours and shortly after carried on with the repairs. I told them to make sure that the whaleback doors were closed and that I could go off the bridge and get my head down. I went below had a nice hot shower, change of clothes and rolled in for the night but not before I read a bit more about gardening.

Not much sleep was had by the crew, what with all the banging and rattling of heavy chain going through the lifting blocks. I went into the messdeck for breakfast which consisted of eggs, bacon, spam fritters, with fresh buns. I downed mine with a fresh brew of coffee. The Galley Boy has not turned to and neither has the Deckie Learner. I think it must have been all the fresh air on the quayside. I put some warm gear on and then checked the mooring ropes. The Skipper said that we should be sailing again before tea.

I pottered about, greasing blocks, davits and then the winch. Lunchtime soon came and went and I went on the bridge after lunch. One of the new crew members, Richard, wanted to learn about chart work and navigation and so we both went through the basics. The engineer popped up and said everything was finished with the broken cylinders and all seems good to sail.

The Skipper was called and after 40 minutes we were on our way again. I took the wheel as we approached Tromso Bridge, I was just told to head for the red light and keep it central. We came through ok and went back to auto steering. The ship began to roll a bit and the pilot informed me it was blowing a full gale out of the fjords and that we were in the best place at this moment in time. The snow began to fall quite heavily and both Clearview spinning windows were working flat out with the heaters on to give us a chance to see anything ahead. The lee side porthole was open and the shoreline could just about be seen two miles off.

The watch soon passed and I handed over to the mate. I went down with my watchmates and the pilot and sat down for tea. Stew and plain duff and I had a bit of the latter in my stew and another bit as a dessert. I asked the cook; 'How's the Galley Boy?' His response was that he had been a waste of space. The Deckie Learner surfaced mid-afternoon and he looked green. He vowed that he would never drink again! I passed the mess and was asked whether

I wanted a game of rummy. I said yes and played for nearly two hours then went and rolled in.

My watch and I called the daymen out at 0700 hours. We were now approaching Trondheim and the snow stopped just after we came on watch at 0300 hours. The fresh smell of busters reached the bridge but it didn't take much to whet our appetites. The watched relieved us and we went down for our breakfasts. We slipped into the messdeck to devour eggs, bacon, sausages, beans and tomatoes.

I am getting fed up of eating this now as it's been four days on the trot. I am looking forward to a piece of fish. I went on the deck with the daymen for an hour just to wash all the oil and slush that came out of the funnels with the leaky liners. I went off the deck just after 1000 hours and took my working gear off, had a nice hot shower and a change of gear. I rolled in at 1030 hours and soon fell asleep. I didn't want any lunch as I was still full from brekkie. Woke up at 1600 hours and had a game of crash with the lads until watcho. This time tomorrow we should hopefully be fishing.

I went on watch at 2300 hours. The sky is ablaze with the Northern lights, lighting the night sky with magical moments with not a cloud in the sky. The houses lit up the mountain sides with the odd moments of traffic on the hillsides. I asked the pilot what time will we be at Honninsvag and his reply was 1300 hours. I went off watch at 0300 hours and I was deado before my head hit the pillow.

Hooray, finally dropped the pilots off at 1400 hours and by 1700 hours orders were given to lift the trawl doors out and to put the net over and cod ends were swung over the side. The shout from the bridge 'LET GO!' and the net started to pull away from the side with the bobbins soon following with the headline thrown manually over the side. The dhan lenos lowered into the water followed by the trawl doors. As we gradually made headway, 300 fathom of warp had been payed out when I shouted 'Last fifty!' The ship slowed down with the messenger hook attached to the forward warp, then' 'LET GO!' was shouted. The fore warp picked up the after warp and together were held into the TOWING BLOCK. 'ALL SQUARE!' was shouted.

I stood by the winch by the break panels whilst they cooled down. then applied shoulder pressure to tighten them. Looking around there were several ships in the area, the St Dominic with her large funnel, the Boston Concord with her streamline body plus about another dozen or so. I just reached about aft when the Skipper shouted; 'Come up for the poison! '(rum). I picked up the bottle and glass. I was told to tell one of the watches to put up the daytime fishing symbol which was a basket. Derek did this for me. I dished out the rum out and had a can of beer before tea. I relieved the Skipper whilst he went for his tea. Twenty minutes later he returned when he told me to get my tea which consisting of braised beef, mashed spuds, carrots and peas followed by, Manchester Tart. I finished my meal, had a smoke in the messdeck, quickly followed by the use of the bathroom and to brush my teeth. I then rolled in for the. night.

Called out at midnight, with the watch telling me that we are hauling at 1230 hours and that the Mates was on the bridge. I had a good night's sleep, dreaming of home but now it's back to reality. I heard the winch being started and dressed quickly with just time for a quick cuppa and a smoke. Whilst on my second cuppa I heard the hammer being used on the towing block with an almighty bang as the block released the warps. I went into the drying room and put my wets on, had a slow stroll to the winch and took up my position for hauling.

Two men were behind the winch using the big wheels that guided the warps on to the barrels evenly. I was told shortly after that it was the last fifty and had a quick look around when I noticed the fish on deck. About a hundred baskets and on the last haul they caught nearly 200 baskets, of what looked like medium cod and haddocks sprinkled here and there. I said to the winchman.' 'You didn't tell me that we had fish left.' The trawl doors came up, followed by the dhan lenos. A 'whoosh' sound was then heard as the cod ends shot to the surface and the rest of the bellies spread out with fish. We pulled the net in by hand till we could get enough net to put the snorkeler on, which we managed, eventually. The Mate came off the bridge to give us a hand and we managed to get the extension to the halving becket. The Mate said to stay forward to undo the cod ends. The first bag came aboard with 40 baskets and 5 more with the same amount. We had to take the middle pound boards out to let the fish run into the area around the washer. The Mate went back on the bridge and shouted down; 'Lift up both the trawl doors. We are going to lay for a couple of hours to clear some fish away.'

It was just beginning to freeze with a sprinkling of snow falling. At times we could see the loom of the land as we were about 30 miles off the North Cape. We were now displaying 2 red lights which meant 'not under command'. This was so that other ships in the area would keep their distance from us, thinking that our nets were foul on the sea bed. Many a time, whilst gutting the fish (not naming anyone) we have been told to go off the deck whilst another ship passed us close by. We went aft for a quick slurp of tea and rolled a couple of cigs and then commenced gutting. A couple of the lads were gutting the fish in the middle whilst the rest stood in the pounds, listening to radio Luxembourg as the weather was calm. Three hours later the Mate shouted down and told us to go aft for a cuppa and that we won't be putting the net over till after breakfast. With the fish being on the large size we managed to put away about 130 baskets which had been good going.

We went aft for a quick cuppa which warmed us through and then straight back into the fish. Gerry stayed aft to tidy the galley and mess for the cook. After about an hour we could smell the aroma of bread and food being cooked. 0600 hours breakfast came and the lads went aft but left two of the watch on deck. They would be relieved at 0630 hours. The Mate came down and told us that we would be shooting the net at 0900 hours and that the fish had slacked off with nobody admitting that they had caught the same amount as us. Just before 0900 hours we washed the decks and ourselves down, leaving about 90 baskets of fish left. We put the net over just after 0900 hours and looked around us on the deck. There must have been at least 30 ships, all fishing in the same area. 1030 hours I was called to the bridge to take the 'poison' round which put a smile on everyone's face. 1145 hours we had finished the fish and washed the decks down which was quickly followed by lunch. Pan of shackles with doe balls which went down nicely. Hauled at 1230 hours with just over 50 baskets of mostly large haddocks this time with a small halibut which went straight to the galley. Another haul before tea and this time we hauled 40 baskets of large cod in the same area and a similar tow.

My watchmates said that they didn't have last night's dram, so when I relieved the Skipper for his tea, I dished out the rum to my watchmates. The Skipper had his tea and said that we had all worked well that day. I had my tea consisting of ham and egg pie, chips, peas and for afters, cornflake tart with a thick custard. I was nearly falling asleep at the table as it had been my first 18 hours for the trip. I went below, took off my smock and socks and I can't remember anything after my head touched the pillow.

After 4 days of successful fishing where we were averaging 200 kit a day, we came fast early morning and lost the full trawl. A mystery ship went across our stern and took our net away. The weather conditions were miserable with heavy snow and light icing. Luckily, we had a spare trawl on the aft gantry. After taking all the remnants away from the bobbins the net was pulled along using the Gilson wire and within the hour the net was put over the side and we resumed fishing. Still, to this day, nobody would admit responsibility for taking the net. The majority of the vessels on our location were from the Humber Region. I'm only pleased that as we were steaming through the fjords, I had been able to make up another pair of cod ends. The lads had made up a spare belly and baiting's. The Skipper shouted out 'Poison!' and I trotted to the bridge. The Skipper praised the crew on how efficient we were to have another spare trawl on the portside. He said that there was no need to make a new trawl up. With a sigh of relief, I told the lads.

Called out at 0900 hours for hauling time. When I heard the screeching of the warps being pulled out, I knew we had just come fast. I quickly put my deck gear on and grabbed a quick cup of coffee and walked towards the winch. The weather was perhaps a 4 or 5 with snow flurries. We were hard and fast on the seabed for what seemed a long time. Eventually we were free of the obstruction. The after door came up, then the fore door appeared both had mud on the shoes. The dhan lenos soon followed and when the cod ends came up it was full of fish. We dropped the bobbins in and then the floats and commenced pulling the net in by hand. We were soon able to use the snorkeler to heave the net up. In the net we had about 100 baskets of large cod which came aboard with three lifts of the cod ends. We also had a small repair in the belly to sort out. I tied the cod ends and went to help with the net mending. I had just picked up the net when the Skipper shouted; 'How long will you be?' I replied; 'About 15 minutes!' In his next breath he shouted; 'YOU WILL GET IF DONE QUICKER IF YOU STOPPED TALKING!'

The net was soon repaired and put back over the side. I popped on the bridge for the morning dram which I took around to the crew. After this I went into the fish pounds and commenced gutting.

Lunch time soon approached and on the menu was pork chops, chips and peas, with halibut soup for starters. As soon as lunch finished it was back into the fish. About an hour and a half later we had finished the fish, when the mate shouted up from the fish room: 'Swing the washer round!' Great news, as we had about 1200 kit on board. We hauled again with 60 baskets and by teatime the decks were clear of fish. I relived the Skipper for his tea and then I had mine. I rolled in soon after my meal, EXHAUSTED!

Rolled out at 1230 hours and we had caught about 30 baskets of fish. It seems that the fish has taken off. Back in the messdeck by 0200 hours and just having a fresh cuppa when we heard a loud bang coming from the engine room which was followed by the fire alarm setting off. As directed, we went to our muster stations and awaited orders. The 2nd Engineer appeared saying that the generator had packed its hand in and oil fumes had set the alarm off. We had a spare generator and shaft generator on board and the Skipper made the decision to haul the net and we are now bound for Honninsvag.

Tied up in Honninsvag at 1300 hours sailed again 1500 hours with the job done. Two leaking piston rings replace and someone's in shit when we get home. Kora came aboard and introduced his son. Same old, same old, with a box of storm lighters which I was told to dish out. He also brought with him some venison, bread rolls and cartons of milk. We also took advantage of putting 40 tons of water onboard. Sailed out of Honninsvag and we headed back to the North Cape. After an hour and a half steaming, we put the net back over the side. 'All square' had been shouted and I took the rum issue around to the crew. On my return I was told to get the forty fathom bridles ready for next haul and I could have the afternoon free.

The Galley Boy, Eric with the Deckie Learner Alf, have been giving Jerry reading lessons in their spare time I believe. Jerry had been brought up as a traveller in his youth and had been a prize fighter. He had been in trouble with the police on many occasions but they gave him a chance by taking him out of town and told not to return, hence he settled in Grimsby as a trawler man.

Teatime soon approached and I relieved the Skipper for his nosh and then I went for mine. Nothing was mentioned about the generator but again that's not my department. Whilst having my tea the crew started hauling the nets. I tucked into homemade burgers, chips and peas with spotted dick for afters. I finished my tea and looked out of the porthole, bag watching and we have about 40 baskets of fish. I had a quick smoke, brushed my teeth and rolled in for the night.

Called out at 0100 hours for hauling time but could have done with another hour. The ship was rolling and pitching. What a difference to six hours ago when it was sunny and calm. I was in the mess having a cuppa and a smoke when I heard through the tannoid telling us to 'knockout'. I put my wet gear on and went out on to the deck. Whilst walking towards the winch a wave came on board and nearly knocked me over. We will have to be careful when hauling in the net. The after door came up followed by the fore door. Soon we were pulling in the net when a cry of 'WATER' was shouted from the bridge and the next thing I heard was a mighty crash as the water came on board which was level with the rail. All the gain on the net was lost. I looked around and all seemed ok with the crew. Nobody was injured but a few of us were wet through. If I wasn't awake when I was called out, I can assure you that I am now. The water cleared away and we commenced pulling the net again. Everything went smoothly and we heaved the cod ends in with about 50 baskets of fish. The Mate screamed out of the bridge window to lift both doors up and that we will be dodging for a while. Most of us went aft and changed into some dry gear. I did the same and put my wet clothes in to the sit-up bath with a cup of OMO wash powder.

We had ten minutes for a cuppa and a smoke then into the fish. We could hear the sound of the wind screeching through rattling's as we settled down gutting and listening to country music. A couple of hours gutting and the fish was all cleaned. Jerry went aft to tidy the galley and make a brew. My watch popped on the bridge for our evening dram and quick yarn to the Mate, who told me that the pilots have been ordered for tomorrow and that we will be shooting the trawl away after breakfast. I left the bridge and went into the bathroom to rinse my clothes in the bath and then I hung them around the immersion heater to dry. Breakfast soon followed and we shot the net away shortly afterwards. Everybody is in high spirits as the trip is nearly over. We are now about 20 miles off the North Cape with only a short run into Honninsvag for tomorrow. I took my boots and smock of and grabbed a couple of hours sleep before we hauled again. The weather has now abated which makes our job a little easier, but not much.

Not had a very good watch below as thinking about going home to spend some time with loved ones. Started hauling at 0230 hours. The Northern Lights were going crazy, zig zagging across the night skies. Hauled and shot the net away with 40 baskets of prime cod. Richard Hardy, our new liver man, has been spending a few hours draining the liver oil and just hoping that we have saved it this trip instead of putting it all back in the sea, as we did last trip! This next haul will be our last for this trip which has been a steady one. We have a few bits of mending and we lost a trawl. The crew has been happy with only one or two arguments that came to nothing. A certain person on here had been a messdeck lawyer and tried a few times to shit stir but nobody has bitten. It is sad really but that's life! Jerry is coming on well with his reading and both parties enjoying it.

Breakfast soon came and went which was a fried fish sarnie in a fresh buster and daddies' sauce. 0900 hours we hauled the nets in with 50 baskets of large cod. Suddenly a voice from the bridge shouted; 'Drop the doors in, lash her up, we're going home!' Twenty minutes later we were heading once more to Honninsvag. I went on the bridge to pick up the morning dram and returned it back to the bridge. The Skipper tells me that my father in-law will be landing the same day as us. We finished the gutting, stowed the washer and put all the deck boards and gratings away. We opened up all the scupper doors and swilled the deck down.

We went alongside to pick up the pilots and pumped some fresh water on whilst we had lunch. We sailed at 1300 hours and Kora came down to let go of the ropes whilst KBS came on to the bridge during my watch. Courses had been set and were going HOME. The Mate came up to report the fish tally to the Skipper. He reported 1,600 kits although we were hoping to land 1700. The catch comprised of 1,200 cod, 300 haddocks and 100 mixed fish. Not bad for a 20-day trip.

I went off watch at 1830 hours and down for my tea. On the menu was venison steaks, fresh mushrooms, tomatoes, with onion rings. The taste still reminds me today of how good the meals were and lots of people didn't have food like this at home. The pilots had a platter of fish between them, rhubarb and custard for afters. Sleep soon beckoned and I awoke at 0200 hours for a nice hot shower and a change of gear. I then reported to the bridge for our watch as we were just approaching Trondheim. There were plenty of boats going about their daily duties.

The Northern Lights were magically flickering across the skies. These magical memories mainly were taken for granted. Jerry keeps going to the chart table, looking at places and muttering the places on the chart. He is trying so hard and well done to the trainees. I met his wife Rose a few months later, saying how far Jerry had come along with his reading and spelling. It must have been very frustrating for him after all these years. Just as we were going off watch we could see the deer on the mountain side in great herds. Snowy the pilot tells us that they would be crossing the water to graze on their winter grounds. When this happens all shipping movements are stopped until they have all finished crossing.

The last of the kippers and smoke fish are for breakfast and the smell of this and fresh bread tickles the tastebuds. I spent a couple of hours after brekkie cleaning the cod ends and putting new cod line meshes on. The cowhides were all in good condition but ordering 4 full hides for next trip along with bluestone crystals to put in the barrels which used for curing hides whilst we are at sea. The atmosphere on the ship was great as we are all going home to our loved ones. I think I might read my farming magazine again.

I awoke at 0700 hours after having a good night's sleep and a bite to eat. We are now approaching Tromso and we will be changing both Pilots, as we go down the south fjords, I was asked to take the helm. Before we could proceed, we had to take her out of auto pilot by changing a couple of valves over which allowed us to use the wheel. I was told to stem the red light and keep it centre. Having passed through the bridge we then started the approach to the quayside and tied up alongside. I asked Eric and Alf if they were going ashore and the answer was our firm 'NO!' They've learnt their lesson from last time!

The new Pilots came on board and with a few words exchanged we proceeded back to sea. A full moon lit up the night sky and the Aurora Borealis were now in full swing. Cars on the shoreline were weaving and winding through mountain side. Jerry came up from the galley with a pot of spesh. For those who don't know, the tea supplied by the company contained large leaves, sugar was added into a large kettle then topped with half a can of Libby's milk. 'Special' is Typhoo tea bags that we obtained [purchased] from the bond. It was made by adding to the large kettle

Typhoo tea bags, a bag of sugar with four cans of Libby's milk. Not everybody would buy this, so they did without.

The end of the watch soon arrived. I went into the messdeck and had a cold fish sarnie with daddies' sauce. I then its brush my teeth and rolled in for the night. I slept like a log and it was nice to wake up naturally which I did at 0900 hours. I had a couple of smokes and a cuppa and took a stroll on the deck. The trawl had been overhauled by the dayman and I just gave them a hand to tie it up along the railings. After lunch the lads will be putting the chloride lime on the deck and leaving it on overnight to be scrubbed off in the morning. During my watch in the afternoon, we 'soogied' the bridge and then gave the brass work the once over, which will be done again before we dock. The bridge mat had been put over the side for an hour and is now laid over the boat deck hand rails to dry. Tea time arrived and on the menu, we had fish and chips, with rice pudding baked in the oven for afters which was delicious. After tea we played cards for a couple of hours and then off to bed for a full night's sleep.

The last couple of days we have been in the fjords. Last night we dropped off both Pilots at a place called Haarstad and we are now on our last day at sea prior to docking. This trip we have seen plenty of wild life and been fishing with all the big boys, Vivaria, Hammond Innes, etc. The scenery has been magnificent, the weather has been fine compared to the ships at Iceland, who have been taking a battering. As we are steaming south, more and more drilling platforms are appearing as they are prospecting for oil or gas. There are plenty of support vessels in attendance and in years to come there will be nowhere to fish. We are approaching Flamborough Head with lots of shipping plying their trade up and down the coast and further afield.

The ship is tidy and all the cabins have been cleaned along with the rest of the accommodation. The fish market prices should be good as there are only 4,000 kits reported for tomorrow's market. We are soon approaching Spurn Light Ship and I was summoned to the bridge to take her down the river. One hour later we were heading through the lock gates to our designated berth which was berth one, with the Northern Queen behind us. I was told to leave the ships wheel amidships as we are now tied up alongside. The Skipper handed me a bottle of brandy and said thank you for everything which I thought was nice of him. I collected my fry of fish and went on to the quayside to meet the wife and travel home. After a full night's sleep, I woke up refreshed and ready for my full English breakfast which I enjoyed. I got dressed to go settle-up down dock.

I got down dock just after midday and we made £24,500.

I had a word with the ships runner who said that I have been asked to go in the Prince Philip with wally Nutton and I said I would because this will mean I have a week ashore. It will be nice to spend time at home with my loved ones. Picked my fish up from Arthur Lacey's (Johnny) and had a few beers in the White Knight, Cairn's, Clee Park then home.

Random Memories - Life at Sea

When a trawlerman left his home to go to sea and said goodbye to their loved ones, it was always uncertain whether or not that they would return home. Most were happy go lucky. Many came from orphanages or prisons. Many having no home life, just wanting to go to work to earn a living. Conditions were not always good what with mountainous seas, severe icing and if the latter we had to work hard to remove the ice for the safety of the ship. It wasn't always doom and gloom though as we made friends for life. We could earn a large amount of money, often working 18 hours a day but before my time there were no watch below. Hauling in the nets in harsh conditions standing knee deep with small fish, with no sign or an end to gutting. Worse still, up all day with maybe two broken trawls. On the plus, you could find yourself working in fine weather just in your shirt sleeves, with large fish, and plenty of sleep. Who else could come home, with a small number of fish to land and end up owing the company money and landing in debt?

Oh, to be a fisherman! Enjoy your fish and chips.

Random Memories - Smells of the Sea

Personal hygiene, on a trawler. was not always a priority for every crew member!

Some people tried while others didn't bother. I sailed with one man in particular, who came away in his suit and wore the trousers all trip. Another person shaved every day. In the deep-water vessels, they carried plenty of water so there was no excuse to be dirty. I had a shower twice a week but in harsh weather a strip wash was taken. I've seen men brushing their teeth with vim or salt as they had forgotten to bring toothpaste. The focsal was a challenge to enter with socks hanging over heater pipes and gutting gloves and mittens on the radiators, may have been smelly at times. Did I notice, you may ask. Not so much, as we all smelt the same.

Random Memories

What other work is there were you used to work 18 hours a day, working away from home. Suffer from sleep depravity, working in minus conditions to put fish on the tables. Heavy icing and watch below would stop to clear any away icing for the safety of the ship and crew. Oh, to be a Trawlerman!

It's a life I chose and loved, although I hated it sometimes to be truthful, but most fisherman would sail again if given the CHANCE!

I would get down dock for about midday, either stroll down or by taxi. I would then pop into the Runners Office for sailing orders and any changes. Climbed up the stairs in Boston's, to either wait your turn or knock on the wicket door. In Boston's a man called Frank had been the cashier. He always seemed happy when you saw him, in or out of a ship, he would give you your settlings then tell you to come down dock the next day and give you a tax rebate not a great deal in returns, mostly around £20.

When you made a decent trip you either went to Burtons or later the American and English Shop, to get measured up for a suit. Mine was usually a four pleated jacket, with 20-inch bottoms in navy blue. After being measured a deposit was left and your suit would be picked up the next trip. If you didn't make a good trip next trip, they often let you have it and pay when you could afford it. Same as Billy Raymond's the hairdresser, haircut on tick lol. When you made a good trip, you had loads of hangers on looking for a Wesley (backhander monies) but if you gave them a treat on a good trip, then on a bad trip you didn't see anyone. If you did, they often crossed the road just to ignore you. This is when the term 'lesson learned' comes to mind, not everybody, just a few. Always made the kids special by taking them to Steele's for tea and a shopping spree on good trips. On bad trips the kids learnt to understand.

12

Boston Concord

Boston Concord – Norway Coast

I came in on the Boston Kestrel and as I had been in her for two years, I thought that I needed a change. I spoke to the Ships Husband and Runner and I was told to leave it with them. I then began to doubt myself and wonder whether I had made a mistake signing off the Kestrel. I thought - 'Let's wait and see.'

I enjoyed the rest of the day as we had made a decent trip as we had a good catch of plaice from the Russian Coast, Cape Charney and Channing. I had never been so cold and as the fish - plaice - hit the deck, it more or less froze solidly. The ones that we could, we gutted and the frozen ones were just thrown in the washer. Not forgetting that on this trip there was plenty of mending and with bare hands holding the wooden needles, all we could do was to lace the nets as mending became almost impossible. We docked with 1,300 kits and made £24,000 and she would be going back to the same grounds.

Well, I had made my decision and I was sticking with it. Afterwards I spoke with the deckie who took my place and he said that he only did the one trip in the Kestrel and wanted to know how I managed being in her for two years. I made no comment.

I settled up and had a few drinks down Freeman Street and then out for tea at Steeles in the Market Place, Cleethorpes.

The next day I went down dock and took my gear off the ship and left it in the offices. I went upstairs for my liver oil money from last trip which I had forgotten to pick up, as you don't get any livers from flatfish. After picking up my monies I was told that I had a tax rebate due. I picked up a forty pounds rebate and was well pleased. It put a smile on my face!

I was about to go downstairs when the Ships Runner and Husband appeared, saying, I would have a week at home and that I would be going in the Boston Concord. So, it looks like I made the right decision, asking for a new challenge. Things were looking up for me and unbeknown to me at the time, two off the crew asked if they could follow me, one being Big Jerry, who did join that trip.

After having a few days in dock, I received a phone call telling me to go down dock and sign on. I remember that it had been a fine day and so I walked down dock to sign on the Concord. The ship was still at the landing quay so I took my gear through the fish market and onto the ship. Before I went aboard, I had been amazed at her size and how she looked sitting in the water. I eventually climbed aboard and noticed that the portside door was open. I shouted out to the watchman who came to the door and let me in. Snowy Richardson was the watchman who was a fisherman who had retired from going to sea, due to ill health. He showed me where my berth was and helped me to get my wet gear and bedding inside. This was duly done and he said did I want a look around and of course I did, so that I could try to familiarise myself and get my bearings.

My cabin was on the portside with a small alleyway leading to two cabins which were mine and the 2nd engineer. Further aft were the officers mess across from the galley and the messdeck. Aft side of that was another alleyway which led down below to the crews' quarters. There was another doorway which led to the bridge and the Skipper's cabin. On walking on the bridge, I was amazed by all the equipment; double radars, sounders, a large radio room just offset and then I noticed the ARKOS steering gear which is the first time that I had come across this type of steering. I began thinking to myself; 'Have I done the right thing?' Snowy had been on this ship before he retired and told me; 'It's piss easy and you will soon get the hang of it!' The chart table had been a good set up with plenty of room available. Lots of ships just had a table and draws but this ship was well set up. Snowy left me to browse by myself and when satisfied that I would be ok I began to descend down the bridge steps. I went down one alleyway to a dead-end. The other way led me to the cook's cabin and storeroom. I shouted Snowy and he just laughed at me and said that I would soon find my way around. Well, let's see! A couple of minutes later the heavy gang came on board to move the ship to the Ice Quay.

I climbed off the ship then I heard Snowy say that he had locked my cabin door for me. I thanked him and walked off the docks with a spring in my steps. I had a pint in the Humber, on to the Albion and then into the White Knight for a few more. Someone asked me why I was happy and I told them that I had just signed on the Concord and he told me that he wouldn't sail across the dock with the Skipper, Billy Balls. However, the person who made these comments didn't remember that we sailed together in the Kestrel when he broke into the bond locker and tried to cause mutiny but hey-ho that's another story. I did not take any notice of comments like these and always judged for myself. In the pub I saw Derek Bartholomew who gave me his fry of fish to take home and he reassured me that if I asked for him on my watch, he would help me settle in which is what he did. I left the White Knight and got a taxi to the Clee Park where I had a couple of beers before going home. In 2 days', time we would be sailing.

Ordered for sailing at 0900 hours but was up by 0700. Having a dozen fags and endless cups of coffee but now the time had come to get ready for the taxi. I put my kitbag by the door and started to pace up and down the lounge looking up and down the street for the taxi. 0930 and the taxi appeared. I ran upstairs and kissed my wife and child goodbye. Back downstairs, picked up my kitbag and into the taxi. Vic Hutchinson was the driver and the only other passenger to pickup was the Skipper who lived of Queen Mary Avenue. A few minutes later we were on the dock approaching the vessel. On leaving the taxi, I didn't realise how high the whaleback was and I climbed up the ladder, with my kitbag over my shoulder heading towards my cabin. I placed my gear on my bunk and went off the ship to Coleridge's to get vitals for the deck which included gloves and knife, as well as some reading material, (gardening) with a few smokes. I climbed the ladder and threw my bits in my cabin. I went aft and met the crew who asked if I wanted a can, I refused as I needed a coffee, my choice. I met the Mate who shook my hand.

The last time I sailed with him I had been the fish room man on the Kestrel. I asked for Bart to be on my watch which he Ok'd and told me to go on the bridge and take the Skipper a mug of coffee. I made one for myself then ventured to the bridge. Skipper was talking to George Sherriff the Radio Operator. The Skipper took his drink off me and when he had finished talking to the Operator the Skipper gave me an induction on the bridge equipment. He demonstrated the steering operation which I had not seen before but I'm sure that I will soon get the hang of it. Looking out the bridge windows I was amazed how big the foredeck and working decks were. I was then asked if I was happy with the bridge equipment and I stated that I will be after my first watch. I was told to go aft and tell the Mate to standby to let go. I returned back to the bridge and stood behind the steering wheel which looked like an aircraft controller. The Skipper gave various orders and we were now leaving the pier heads and out into the river Humber. On passing the Burcom (buoy) I was shown how to put the steering into automatic and we soon reached the Spurn Light Ship where the course was set NNE.

After getting relieved from the bridge, I went to my cabin to get changed and put my gear away. Whilst doing so big Albert popped his head into my cabin to say hello! I first sailed with him in the Renown and he told me that he was the foreman dayman and if I wanted a tour of the deck etc. to let him know. With the weather being fine off we went. The first thing I noticed was that everything was in a neat and tidy order. There were labels displaying the different sizes of rope and wire work. The cod ends were brand new, with plenty of spare gear made up. After passing the winch I was informed that when we shoot the trawl away the winch is shipped up and reversed off. The time was approaching lunchtime and I hadn't had anything to eat yet. There was a big pan of shackles, which I soon tucked into. When I finished my lunch, I grabbed a couple of hours sleep. Tea time soon came upon us and on the menu was a mixed grill which I had and then onto the bridge to take my first watch. Jerry and Bart were my two watchmates and I soon familiarised myself with the surroundings and machinery. There were plenty of ships. and platforms. The sky was beautiful and clear and we had to safely navigate around a few vessels nearby. Plenty of phosphorus in the water, with. a clear evening sky we travelled onward to the Norwegian Coast.

Nearly two days away. During the morning we finally put the washer and deck boards in place. The weather had freshened up previously but please to say that it has now abated. The sky's a light blue with sunshine, only thing that's around are the seagulls and we often see puffins and razorbills. We do see a lot of wildlife including porpoises, dolphins and many species of whale. The bond had been issued which included cigarettes, tobacco including papers, tin of Quality Street for home, plus a tin of chocolate coated Brazil nuts. I was issued with a case of Red Bass Ale. We all had a Colman's mustard jar full of rum issued just before lunchtime, which gave me an appetite.

The cook 'Budgie' I would class as a basic cook with no frills to his food but it always tasted like grannies cooking and was always pleasant. He carried a large tape to tape recorder with a fine mixture of music. I have known him a few years as he lived local to me. Twenty-four hours later we are approaching Lodigen Pilot Station to take on two pilots to take us through the fjords. We had a spare cabin where the pilots could sleep during the time on board. Big Jerry has come on in leaps and bounds with his reading and writing. In the messdeck he reads out aloud from magazines etc but nobody will tell him to shut up. Who would be brave enough? He had asked the runners which ship I was in so he could sail with me. Still, lots of snow on the mountain sides seeing as its now March time. During the evening and early mornings, the skies are being lit up with the northern lights. My only wish is that we had modern-day phones and cameras we have today during this time. We could have recorded our times at sea.

Breakfast time arrived and we had the last of the smoked fish, haddock and kippers, digested with fresh busters and a fresh cuppa. The mates going on watch and I'm not needed on the deck. I took my leave off the mess and went below to catch up on my gardening magazines.

We sailed after eight hours as we were waiting for the reindeer to migrate. The weather's getting colder and it is beginning to snow heavily. Everywhere we look is like a picture postcard. Tromso Bridge is well lit up. We are now heading underneath and proceeding North towards the fishing grounds. The news is that a lot of ships are catching lots of fish at the White Sea. I am looking forward to seeing how this ship performs fishing. When I went on watch, it was been a pleasure to use the new equipment and feel the ship running through the water with such power. We have been averaging about 15 knots. Teatime soon approaches and looking forward to a couple of hours playing cribbage after tea. Tonight, may be the last time we will be able to play as we will be soon on the fishing grounds.

We have been steaming for 18 hours through the fjords without any more hindrance. Dropped the pilots off at 1830 hour and the watch below have been set. I had my tea which was a lovely roast beef meal with carrots, sprouts, mashed tatties with an onion duff followed by treacle pudding and custard. Rolled in at 1900 hours and was just about to bob off, when I heard the trawl doors being lifted. The next thing I remember were the words; 'Hauling time!' I got dressed into my gear, had quick sip of tea then put my wet gear on and proceeded towards the main deck. The Mate had been at the winch and I took my post at the after door. Last fifty was called, the short mark was called 2 minutes later. The after door surfaced and the chain was passed through the brackets which was then secured to a large hook. Slack was given, the bridle pennant was released from the backstrap, the fore door had done the same, both bridles were heaved on which brought the dhan lenos to the surface. The headline rope was taken to the winch, the same with the 'bang bang' gear wire. Both were then heaved together. The bobbins came over the rail quickly followed by the headline.

Now the work really started as we manually pulled the net in. Hand over hand together, we worked as a team, until finally we could push the net together at the rail to enable us to use beckets which in turn pulled the net in until we came to the cod ends. The mate and myself decided to use the halving becket to bring the fish in. Eventually the bag of fish came over the side and was contained by the bag ropes. I ventured forward to untie the cod line which had a reef knot and was tucked into the end of the cod line. I took the rope out of its loop and took a to a couple of turns off the end then shouted to lower the cod ends down, I then released the last hitch which discharged the fish. We had caught about 50 baskets of mostly large cod and haddock.

Not bad for the first haul. We cast the net back over and straight into the fish after a quick smoke and a mouthful of tea leaves (those that know). Settled down gutting the fish with country music playing over the speakers, Slim Whitman, yodelling!

We are laid gutting after a successful night of fishing. Having to pace myself with the first eighteen-hour shift of the trip. The weather's not so good and the ship is rolling quite heavily but it makes things easier with the large cod being thrown into the fish washer. Everyone is in a good mood after having a couple of extra tots of rum. It's mid-afternoon and teatime will soon be upon us. On a good note, a few of the crew have their own gardening magazines which we share and discuss with each other when we have some spare time. Rose bushes and melons are quite a topic.

Rolled out at midnight to a gale of wind. Both trawl doors have been dropped in and we are slowly dodging, head to wind. How refreshing walking on the deck having just woken up, with what felt like a million hailstones hitting you at 30 miles an hour. We relieved the watch below and settled into the fish. Music blaring out to the sounds of 'Stand by Your Man' etc. I liked listening to this type of music generally but most of Country and Western is about doom and gloom. Shouted up to the bridge to change the music and the Mate obliged with the Beachboys etc.

After a couple of hours, we were told to go and get a hot drink and a smoke. The time now was nearly 0300 hours and we had about 20 baskets of large cod left. Just as we were almost aft, there was an almighty crash. A rogue wave had come onboard and the starboard rail lifted up and smashed the pound boards as well as the jockey boards. These were all floating on the deck and we could have all been killed or maimed. The mate had called the Skipper out and he then came down to us and informed us to go back on the deck. The Skipper will run down the wind enabling us to secure the decks. The engines gained speed and the ship turned around. We were given the order to go on deck and be aware of the conditions.

There were no fish left to gut and half of the deck boards had smashed like matchsticks. It took us about 20 minutes to put the boards back. The broken boards were thrown into the forward bins and we commenced lashing the trawl down using both the forward and after Gilson wires. All the time we were working, big seas were following us and we were surfing through the water. When the job was completed, we went aft. The fish room hatch was water tight and the doors were all battened down. I was the last man aft on the deck and I closed the door behind me. Then using the tannoid system I contacted the bridge and informed the skipper that we were all inside. I was told to take my wet gear off and pop to the bridge. On arrival I was given a bottle of rum to dish out to the deck crew only Someone was looking over us that night!!

Oh, to be a fisherman, working in all conditions, often working in terrible seas, heavy weather, freezing conditions, not ashamed to have cried when hands and body had been ice cold. Standing hours on end gutting fish or mending nets. Did we complain? Not really, just gritted our teeth and got on with things. On the other hand, working with great mates for life, seeing plenty of wildlife, visiting many ports with different cultures and not forgetting the scenic views.

Oh, to be a fisherman!!

Up to our necks again with large cod and it has been like this for three days. The weather has improved but most of the crew are on a downer. It's nearly 1100 hours and the rum issue has been dished out, washed down with a can of beer. Lunch today is halibut soup with hot busters to dunk into the liquid. Most of the crew sent a telegram home. I sent mine wishing the wife a Merry Christmas and looking forward to being at home with the family.

The fish tally this morning 1400 kit and this time tomorrow we shall be making our way home to land for the New Year's market. Hauled just after lunch with 60 baskets of fish, now we have a total of 150 baskets to gut and put away. Three hours later all fish put away, the decks washed, this is the first time they have been clear in 4 days. Hauled before tea with 30 baskets of mainly haddocks with a sprinkling of large cod. Steaming towards land during tea time which was turkey and all the trimmings, pigs in blankets, sage and onion stuffing followed by Christmas pudding with brandy custard which had a kick to it. The Skipper came back from tea and said one more haul and we are going in. We will be going alongside Honninsvag, taking on fuel and water. Oh, what a relief!

The trips been quite a challenge with a few decent holes mended but only changed the trawl once. We had a one ended job when we parted a bridle (cables), locked doors, just the one time, shooting against the tide. The weather has been up and down. Smashed a few boards up, with bent gratings, other than that it's been good. Feel really proud of being the Bosun on here. It's a lovely sea ship with a good crew, now that they have accepted me, prior to saying we don't do it that way. They now know I had different methods of working on the deck and that they work. I filled my stomach with a lovely meal then thanked the cook who is usually an unsung hero working every day in all weathers. I left the officers mess, brushed my teeth, searched for my gardening magazines, now I have a dozen, gives you some ideas. How the other half lives lol!

Tied up in Honninsvag just after breakfast and we are not sailing till 1300 hours. Kora came aboard (agent) with his son with usual for visit, lighters, meat, bread buns, etc. I got a yarn bent on with him and he asked if I wanted a tour around Honninsvag which I said yes. General town with a few shops, a couple of cafes to be seen whilst travelling through and he took us up the hillside and to my surprise there was a ski jump nearly to Olympic standards. He asked if I wanted a go but I just grimaced at the pair of them. I was then driven to his office/warehouse where I noticed a lot of trawling gear with ships names on the labels, especially coils of rope etc. Someone has been trading on the ships. Quite a few names were there, Hull and Grimsby boats. After leaving his workplace I was then taken back to the ship. I was given a carton of cigarettes wrapped in brown paper.

Once onboard I grabbed hours sleep before sailing. We have now let go from the quayside just before 1400 hours with 2 pilots on board KBS plus another pilot I had not come across before. We are now heading south towards the fjords. I went to my cabin after letting go and saw the package on my bed. On opening I discovered they were Zobrana, Russian cigarettes. I lit one and it stunk the ship out. I shouted down the alleyway for someone to take the cigarettes but no one offered to take them. I think I gave them to the pilot boat.

We are now approaching the lock gates, having been at sea for 19 days, dock to dock plus a few hours waiting for the reindeer to cross the fjords before we reached Tromso going North. Looking back over the last few days, coming home through the fjords, it is always spectacular not just mountains and different landscapes but watching the different colours of the night skies giving us a different display every time we see it. The pilots were dropped off at Lodigen, with the pilot cutter taking them off us but not before they filled their faces with a fish breakfast and they took the leftovers with them. The trawl had been repaired, changed a few bobbins and footropes. I concentrated on the cod ends, put a new bottom half in, changed most of the cowhides, complete with new cod line meshes. The trawl secured to the rail and prepared for the next voyage. On leaving the Norwegian Coast we saw a lot of longlines plying their trade. They often appear in the areas we are trawling. Then the fishery boats move us on out of the areas.

Twelve hours from leaving the coast we start coming across more and more drilling rigs popping up, with the night skies lit up as they start burning the gasses off. The atmosphere on the ship is sky high and the Mate reckons we should turn out about 1,400 kits and market prices are good with only three boats landing, two deep-water [Iceland], ourselves, and a couple of catboats. The night before we docked, we had a few beers and a game of cards. I finished cleaning my cabin before my last watch. I put all my gardening magazines away from prying eyes. Maybe use as swaps next trip.

As we are going through the lock gates the Skipper says that him and the mate are having a couple of trips off, all to do with tax and the financial year. Tied up alongside, the quayside berth number 2, wheel amidships and that's me finished. Not before I was given a bottle of brandy. The Skipper thanked me for the trip and I proceeded off the bridge. Picked my gear and fish up. Looking forward to seeing the family etc. and chill for a couple of days before we sail again.

Landing day. Turned out 1,450 kits and made £23,600.

Now I have a week off before we sail again. Taking the wife down Freeman Street. Having a couple of beers, then to Marks and Sparks, followed by the Peabung for a fish dinner.

Missing the Festive Season

Going to sea during the festive season was always hard to bear. Leaving your wife and children was the most difficult. Money was often tight and the men had to go to sea to pay their bills. The fishing conditions, especially at this time of year with bad weather, stormy seas and ice were particularly harsh.

I have known the weather to be so bad that as soon as we reached the fishing grounds the ships had to shelter in the fjords. However, on some occasions the weather could be good and with an abundance of fish. This meant coming home with a good catch and hopefully a good market and being able to earn plenty of money. Lots of lads stayed at home and at these times we would get what we called 'Christmas crackers' signing on these fishermen who couldn't get regular work, for whatever reason. Another bonus was if you had a decent cook.

My children never liked me being away at sea during these times but I always tried to make it up to them by having our own Christmas when I came home and letting them have a treat from the 'sales' when we had proper sales!

For us fishermen being at sea during the festive season was like any other day at sea. We just knuckled down to things and concentrated on the tasks we had to do which was hopefully to catch fish. I had always prepared myself for being away. The hard part was leaving the family at home but once in the taxi, home life was put to the back of our minds. We were all in the same boat. The weather was mainly poor at this time of year but then again, we could have Indian Summers where we had all come home suntanned when it had been freezing at home.

We still had Christmas dinners but without the fuss. It was always turkey and all the trimmings then back to the pounds to clean the fish. I always knew that my wife and kids were ok as her family all came together as one, whilst I was away. When we came home, we had our own time together!

Christmas and New year were never a good time to be at sea. Many a time we have been battened down with gales of wind which included snow and ice. I used to say; 'I will stay at home next year!'. However, that was not always possible if finances were low, so then it would be another Christmas at sea on the cards. Demand for fish was at a premium at this time of the year to keep the factories supplied and the markets were therefore good. I never mentioned the conditions to my loved ones. We just knuckled down and got on with our job without any complaints. Usually, we made a decent living this time of year but this was not always the case.

When we came home every docking day would be like a honeymoon and landing day was like Christmas day for the kids.

Random Memories

Another trip, after landing day (Boston Concord) I went down dock for my liver money and was informed by the ships husband that the Concord was going in to drydock for a mini fit out [a 10-day wonder] and would I be willing to go in her with a skeleton crew including Skipper, Mate, Bosun, Chief. Cook and three ABS sailing breakfast time tomorrow and that I would be home by tea time. The wife wasn't impressed but it had to be done. Up next day and a taxi down dock.

We sailed at 0730 hours and tied up in Blyth about 1600 hours. The ship went straight into the drydock and by 1730 hours we were told that we had to stay onboard for the night which is what we did. At about 1830 hours a few of us were lifted off the ship in a basket using a crane and were told we would be lifted back on later. On the quayside there was a pub, I think that they called it the Dun Cow and we had a few beers, a phone call then back to the ship. We were told to call back in the pub when we were leaving just after lunch time. I had a good night's sleep and woke up for breakfast. I collected the few personal items I had aboard and the coach to take us home had been ordered for 1300 hours and when 1100 hours came, we were lifted off by the crane into the pub for a couple of beers etc.

The time came to get in the coach when the gaffer gave us some hot pukka pies, a few sarnies and a few cans of ale and soft drinks. We said our farewells then travelled home and arrived just before teatime. In the evening I had a few drinks in the local and then went down Cleethorpes. The next morning, I popped down dock and picked my money up for taking the ship to Blyth. Outside our office stood Charley Ward, who was the runner for B.U.T.'s and I was asked to do a favour and would I go North Sea in the Ross

Jaguar with Shelly Stokes. I asked our runner and was told that it would not be a problem.

Anyway, I joined the Ross Jaguar, sailed just before lunch, and just after tea we shot the nets away, quarter ropes and chains were used to catch the fish. No washer, everything was laid on the deck, mainly sand, curly weed and searching on your hand and knees for the fish. No watch below, with the net only being towed for a maximum of 3 hours. After a week's work I think that we had 300 kit and honestly, I have never worked so hard in my life, I take my hat off for the North Sea Tigers.

I ran off the ship faster than a cheetah!

12 + 1

Boston Concord

I have been enjoying extra time at home, celebrated the night away in the White Bear and saw the New Year in at the White Knight. The usual thing with the idiots out thinking they could drink but hey let them get on with it. I hardly remember getting home as there were no taxis to be had and so I walked home. I then had a ham sarnie, I think and awoken with the hangover from hell but all I got from the wife was that I'm too greedy on the Whisky shots!

Had a hair of the dog which was a double shot of Bells and felt like boking but managed to keep it down. The wife then shouted breakfast was ready. Really! Didn't think I could eat it but after 20 minutes I had finally eaten it all. Now I'm feeling better. I then washed it down with a Bombay oyster (raw egg in milk). Now I'm ready for another sesh but not bothering as we are going to visit the family today and I'm sure I will have a few noggings to keep me going. It's now elevenish and getting ready to go out. I then saw my kitbag ready for the next trip under the stairs but hey-how I have four more days before we are sailing again. Stepped out the front door a few neighbours were out wishing everyone a Happy New Year.

Final preparations getting my kitbag packed. The wife has put a few bits to eat and some goodies off Freeman Street Market. I went around to say goodbye to the family and spent most of the day chilling. Never went out the day before sailing. Since I got married my priorities are now my family, not like I did when I was single and carefree.

Married life suited me, particularly knew this as when I first set eyes on Cheryl. I knew that this person would make me happy. It took me a while changing from a single person to being married man, especially now that I have a young son to consider. My responsibilities make it harder going to sea but fishing had been the life that I chose to do. Not much on the television so it's an early night as we have been ordered for sailing at 0530 hours.

I was picked up at 0630 hours by taxi and taken straight down dock. I climbed on the ship and I didn't need any stores and went to put my gear in my cabin. I was summoned to the bridge to let go and after taking her down the river I was relieved by the Mate who took the watch.

After coming off the bridge I unpacked my kitbag and put my treats away, along with my acquisition of gardening and wildlife magazines. My old ones are ready for swaps during the voyage. Bonzo [Mate] came to my cabin just before tea time and asked how things are with the crew. Not a lot of people got on with him but he was a person who didn't like layabouts and whifflers. I sailed with him in my start up years as fish room man and he paid good money out of his own pocket. He asked me the information on the workings of the ship with the winch etc. told him I will give him a rundown in the morning.

Tea time approached and I went into the officers' mess for tea which consisted of a mixed grill, sausage, gammon, black pudding, onion rings fries, and a portion of steak, tomatoes topped with a mushroom sauce. Budgie had excelled himself tonight. I couldn't eat the Manchester tart but I sneaked a bit away and put it in my cabin. I closed the door and proceeded to the bridge. The Skipper [Andy Jensen] handed the watch over to me and we were just passing Whitby Headlands. The weather was a southerly force seven and the ship was sailing with a gentle roll now and again, unlike the ships heading south, with the whalebacks flicking seas over the breakwater and onto the main deck.

The weather had been too bad to put the washer up although the yoyo had been rigged. The Skipper came back from his tea and asked if I had my tobacco with me which I produced. Without warning he opened my tin, put enough baccy in his mouth to make 20 fags and started to chew it. I didn't make that mistake again! The Operator came onto the bridge and radio room then passed the ships schedule to the Skipper with both the weather conditions and what fish our ships were catching. The Skipper told me but at this time I was not really interested as we have another 2 days to go before we reached the grounds. We are averaging 17 knots speed and we have more if needed. The skies are beginning to clear, and we could see about 10 miles ahead of us with the naked eye.

As we are leaving the coastline, we are now getting glimpses of the stars and occasionally a shooting star would appear over the horizon. 2100 hours the Operator went to roll in and the Skipper went at 2130 hours after putting the night orders into the log book. A few herring gulls are flying effortlessly alongside, looking for morsels to eat. 2245 hours watches were called. The Mate came up first and pulled me aside asking queries on a couple of the crew. I just told him it is not my place to say and Bonzo appreciated that I wasn't a grass. I went off the bridge, made a pot of drinking chocolate and took this to my cabin where I had my Manchester tart with my drink. I then brushed my teeth and rolled in for the night.

After a good night's sleep and feeling refreshed, I went for my breakfast before I went on watch. I had a nice bowl of porridge with a hot buster lathered in margarine and treacle syrup, running out the bun and down my chin. I finished my breakfast and went on watch. We were approaching. Buchaness where there were quite a lot of small fishing boats running up and down the coastline plying their trade. Just ahead of us were a few supply boats running towards the Shetland's with deck loads of oil and gas essentials. Just after 0900 hours the Skipper came on the bridge and said that I could go down on the deck, where Bonzo had been waiting for me to show him around the working deck.

The daymen were busy putting the washer and boards up. The trawl and cod ends were all done going home last trip and just needing a new cod line which I had already prepared to put in this morning. I went down the fore hold where the spare nets were stored along with the bobbins and rubbers. I explained the working of the winch and that you shot the gear away, shipped up on here and that the winch noise sounded like a tank engine. I was about to go aft when the Skipper shouted Bonzo. We carried on aft to get a fresh brew. After my cuppa which I took on the bridge with me, I discovered the area to be filled with the deck and engineers waiting their turn for the bond issue. Just before lunch I received mine along with a nogging of rum and a case of beer. I took my compliment of fags and baccy along with papers and Swan Vestas, a mixture of sweets and a packet of Camay soap. Lunchtime time came and at 1230 hours I was relieved off the watch and went for my lunch, which was stew and dumplings, followed by a lay down on my bunk for an afternoon siesta.

Called out just before dinner and told that we will be docking soon in Torshavn which is in the Faroe Islands. I had a quick smoke then onto the bridge. It seems that we have developed radar issues during the morning time and I was told to get the mooring ropes prepared for docking. We tied up about 1300 hours and as we approached the quayside the Skipper's father and son [Andy's brother] were there to greet us. They came onboard and went up to the skipper's cabin. The radar man came onboard and checked things over and after one hour's work, he was finished. He gave me a paper with his name and company without the amount it had cost.

The Skipper popped his head on the bridge and told me that he is off ashore and he would be back in 2 hours and that we would be sailing straight away. I went for a quick stroll on the quay and saw the locals fishing with their rods and catching plenty of Sul locks, which were a nightmare fish to us as they took an eternity to gut when we were catching them. After nearly 3 hours the Skipper came back with a couple of boxes which were directed towards the galley. Fifteen minutes later we were on our way towards the fishing grounds. At teatime I was relieved by the Mate and went down for my tea and the Skipper followed me. For tea we had shepherd's pie, mixed vegetables with an onion duff. I finished plating my meal when the cook appeared with a sheep's head on a platter. I asked the Skipper if I could be excused which he granted. I took my dinner into the crew's mess to eat. At nearly 1900 hours the Skipper popped his head into the mess and beckoned me to follow him. He stood outside the freezer with a large grin on his face pointing into the fridge and to my amazement there were more sheep heads, dried fish, whale blubber and razz fish [which smelt rotten]. 'Do you want to taste any?' he asked. I just looked at him and he presumed my answer was 'NO!!'

I retreated to my cabin, had a nice hot shower and rolled in for the evening. At 0400 hours the next day we put the net over for the first tow of our voyage. My watchmate Spearpoint is a little worried as he's going fish room man this trip - he has only been a deputy prior to this trip but I'm sure that he will be ok.

Leaving the land and we don't have the Internet, television or radio in the messes. The only news we hear is on radio 4 with the fishing forecast and the Archers to entertain us. On a Sunday morning we had Wilfrid Pickles ('Give him the money Mable') and Sunday evening the Black and White Minstrel Show. We didn't have any luxuries but we did have the Northern Lights for entertainment.

Just after breakfast I ventured on the deck for the first haul of the trip. The weather has deteriorated and is now near to gale force, running from the north. The seas are 5 metres high with the wind at this time about 40 knots and the snow showers don't help things. Times like these all you wanted was to be sat at home snuggled up with your loved ones. Now back to reality.

The after door came up first then the fore door, both hung on a chain, links released then heaving on the bridles, as the dhan lenos were coming up you could see the bubbles surfacing from the cod ends area. They appeared with a red ruddiness which was the tell-tale sign of squaddies. The bobbins came inboard, followed by the floats, now it was time to pull the net in by hand. Both hands in the net pulling in unison, then kneeling on the net to trap it, then hands moving back into the net, then carrying on pulling. Everything was going ok when a voice shouted 'WATER!'. Immediately we stopped pulling the net and held on to the handrail. Luckily no great amount of water came aboard and we proceeded to pull the net in again. Once we had the aid of the winch the Skipper gave a quick kick astern to fill the cod ends with fish.

The first bag came aboard, followed by four more bags full, 98% of which were red fish with a few haddocks. The Skipper laid the ship whilst we threw the red fish into the washer and the chaffed haddocks were thrown back over the side. After an hour or so we dropped the doors in and lashed the trawl down. We are now heading towards Largeness on the East side of Iceland. The journey will take us about 12 hours.

Went on watch at 1230 hours. I must say what a fine ship we are in during this heavy weather just riding through the water. We are just steaming up the East side of Iceland. We passed a couple of ships going home and we are now heading to the North Cape as there's been no fish at Largeness, Melaka or at Red Head. The Skipper has been talking to his Faroese friends and they are having decent catches and that's where we are heading now. Catching 60 to 70 baskets for 3-hour tows. We are about 8 miles off the land and there's plenty of snow on the shorelines and mountains. Just behind us there are other ships heading north. I will be glad when we are fishing and settled down once more. During the afternoon the weather dropped away, and just before tea I dished the morning dram out to those who were up. Teatime soon arrived and the Skipper relieved me. He asked did I have my baccy on me. 'No' was my reply! Not getting caught again!

Called out at 0400 hours for shooto. Had a quick smoke and a fresh cuppa. I heard the ship easing down in speed and we all ventured on to the deck to a light covering of ice. The net was frozen. Let go of all the lashings and we then heaved both trawl doors over the rail. Next, we checked the cod line which had been covered by the cowhides and the, yoyo hook was put into the lifting chain. The order was given by the Skipper to lift the cod ends and put over the side and the net followed slowly, mainly in a heap but soon formed its shape in the water. The bobbins went over followed by the floats. We were just about to lower the Dhan lenos when the fore door man shouted that the bridles were stranded. I took a look myself and it's a good job it had been noticed. We put chains and slips on the shackles, pulled the bridles off and changed them out. Eventually we shot the trawl and we were now fishing again. Before we came off the deck, we stowed the old bridles for dumping at a later date.

We took our gear off as it was fast approaching breakfast time. Time for a quick smoke then into the officer's mess for my meal which was spam fritters, eggs, beans, with a bowl of porridge for starters. The Skipper came for something to eat and told me to tell the fore-door men to pop on the bridge for an extra dram of rum. What they spotted could have cost us dearly. After my breakfast Bonzo came off the bridge saying the ships are averaging 50-60, baskets for 3-hour tows. I eventually went to my cabin and started to read my gardening magazines.

Called out 20 minutes before hauling time. I went aft to the oilskin locker to put on my frock and thigh boots together with my muffler, hat and gloves. All prepared for hauling. I managed to get a hot cuppa down me and an endless supply of fags before I ventured out on to the deck. As soon as I stepped onto the deck the amount of steam that came out of my mouth indicated how cold it was. At this time, it was minus 5-6 and luckily with calm seas otherwise we would ice up. The decks were slippery and we had to watch our footing, so we did not slip. 'Last 50!' shouted up to the bridge. 'Hold the short mark!' came the reply. This is when the ship would do a 360 degree turn when the doors came up followed by the net etc. with about a hundred baskets of really nice medium cod, a splattering of haddocks and a few plaice mixed in.

This is what it's all about. Tied the cod line and the net went over without a problem. Took my position in the winch house and payed the warps over until we reached the needed depth. We secured both warps into the towing block, went into the mess and tried to roll a cigarette but my beard had been frozen and now in the warmth I started to defrost with the moisture falling on to my hands. One of the crew gave me a tailor made and I popped on the bridge for the morning dram which I took round. I gave the fore doorman an extra dram but he gave me half. The dram glass used to be an empty Colman's mustard jar which turned out to be a decent size. I returned the rum to the bridge and took my place in the pounds, to gut the fish. Lunchtime soon approached which turned out to be a nice thick chicken broth to warm us through. We hauled at 1400 hours. The decks were clear of fish prior to hauling and we caught about 60 baskets. Another haul before tea. I relieved the Skipper for his meal and afterwards had mine. Now it was time for some SHUT EYE!

I was called out at midnight saying we are just shooting the net with 200 baskets of cod on the deck. I had a warm drink, a smoke and rolled a couple of fags for the pounds. The time came to go on the deck where I found the catch was all very large cod. I asked for the whiffling stick and sharpened my knife. When gutting the fish, they were mostly full of roe or chicklings. The roe was saved in a basket, as were the livers, in a separate basket. After a couple of hours, the fish were down the fish room. We then started to bag up the roes in sacking bags and we passed the roes down the fish room. After completion half a basket of mixed were handed up for the galley. Fish always tasted better after it had been laid on the ice for at least 12 hours. The fish was taken aft into the galley storeroom.

I took my gear off and waited for my watch mates and went on to the bridge for our evening rum issue. My watch mates had there's and I stayed behind and had a quick chat to the Mate. I had previously sailed with Bonzo when he was mate with Tommy Whitcombe when I had an accident, using the tackle block, whilst using the heavy lifting combination becket. As I attempted to put it into the eyepieces, it suddenly came out and cut me above my right eye. I caught the block and put it in again without a problem. Bonzo let go of the cod line and then the job stopped whilst I was taken on the bridge. The mate followed, Whitcombe looked away and told the mate to stitch the wound up, which he did. I was given a dram and sent back on the deck and carried on with my duties. Years later, when the fishing days had finished, I often had a few beers with him.

After having my dram, I was told that we would be hauling again in half an hour and to ask the watch to bring a pot of tea for him when it was made, please. He was a very polite man but don't upset him, as he had a quick temper. Whilst we were hauling the nets, we became one man short for a while whilst the galley and messdecks were cleaned out. Sometimes Alf, the greaser, would do this for us. We started to haul the net up but as we were pulling the net in, large cod were escaping from the belly head. As we had brought the broken part in, we used the long haws and short hawks to bring the floating fish on board. We managed to get a few. We had about 60 baskets of the large cod again. We cut the bad part of the net that had ripped and put a new piece in. From hauling, to putting the net back over, took about an hour in total. It's good when you have a crew that can mend as it makes life so much easier.

Soon breakfast came upon us which was nice piece of haddock, cooked in flour, with fresh busters and a lovely cuppa. After half an hour, for mealtime, it was back to gutting the fish. We had another 3 hauls then teatime came upon us which was liver and onions, mashed tatties with a plain duff. Oh, the joys of food at sea. Lots of fishermen could not afford food like we had but Boston's were renowned for providing good food. Feeling shattered! I crawled into my bunk and sleep soon took over.

Over the last few days, it's been non stop. We have caught plenty of fish and changed the trawl twice. The last time we only recovered the bobbins and a few cans (floats). We have also repaired one and made another one up. We have two full trawls and I will have to make a pair of cod ends up when we get the chance. This trip we have been thrown all over the place with the inclement weather. Northerly winds that chill you to the bone.

Jerrys been in trouble twice and both times Bonzo has broken it up. The Radio Operator took a morning dram round for the crew and he said to Jerry, 'Get to the back of the queue, I'm giving the workers there's first.' Well, Jerry bopped him one. He broke his nose and jaw. We put the operator ashore in Isa fjord. On another occasion the cook gave a snide remark and Jerry grabbed him like a rag doll. He didn't mouth off again.

The weather has now calmed down a bit and we are averaging 60 baskets of cod for 4-hour tows. We have seen quite a bit of ice 30 miles off the cape and a few ships have been towing alongside it and are catching the same amount as us. We have about 1.400 kit on board with 3 more days to go before we go home. Just hauled again with 50 baskets, shot the net away and just taken the morning dram round. Really looking forward to going home this trip.

Bloody knackered as I have been up since midnight chopping ice. Using crocodile spanners, knocking out hammers and steel tubing's. We had been dodging in to Isa fjord due to a bad forecast. The net had been scrambled aboard with the cod ends covering about 50 baskets of fish. Took the ice off the foredeck and mast first, followed by the bridge and finally the aft mast and casing area. We are now under Rittur Hook and we have dropped the anchor. To hear the wind screeching through the mast and rigging is nearly piercing our ears. After 6 hours of chopping ice the watches were started again. The Mate took the anchor watch to give the Skipper a break and to get a bit of shut eye. Breakfast was soon upon us. With a few tired faces after all the clearing away of the ice we had breakfast then went to the fish pounds moving the cod ends off the fish. We started to gut the fish. Lots were decent to clean but a few was like cutting into cardboard. Cleaned just over two thirds when the mate shouted; 'Lash the cod ends down and come off the deck.' It was now snowing quite heavily. We waited until the fish room men had finished then battened down the hatches. The snow was settling on the decks but thankfully there was no ice. Left the donkey running (water hose) so that it didn't freeze over. I took all my work gear off, oilskin frock, muffler, gloves, smock, jumper [with no sleeves in] and then lifted each thigh boots off.

The cook let us in the galley a few at a time to warm up. I just wanted a hot drink and a few smokes. This time away a few of the lads were quite snappy with each other. I was just on my second smoke when Bonzo called for me on the ships tannoid to pop on the bridge for the rum issue. The smiles were soon back on the crews faces. Took the bottle back on the bridge and was told that later in the day we would be steaming southerly and going towards the Tannoid Hoof and the Horns to finish off. The Belgaum and the Boston Phantom, have no icing up to report.

I had my lunch which was a big pan of shackles with 20-minute floaters and fresh busters. Rib clinging food! I went on the bridge just before 1600 hours and we lifted the anchor and ventured out of Isa fjord and headed South along the East Coast. We did a bit of heavy rolling at first but then settled down with the wind on our quarter. The wind was North West and we were on a Southerly course. I am ready for my tea and watch below. I can't remember much about rolling as I must admit I was totally exhausted. We are now on our tenth day of fishing and mostly working eighteen hours a day.

Eighteen hours on and what a difference in the weather. The seas are now calm with no wind, with one or two snow flurries. We have had two hauls both with 50 baskets of prime fish consisting of large haddock, medium cod and a few langoustines mixed in as well. This time tomorrow this trip will be all over. It has not been a hard trip but challenging all the same. I can't praise the crew enough but what a team and that's what a good crew is, working together in somewhat harsh conditions. Sometimes you wished that you worked ashore and home every night but we are a special breed who thrived on adventures. Working ashore would be boring and sometimes the rewards were high and times when we had bad trips landing in debt but we always went back and tried again.

We are just in the process of hauling, doors are up with the code ends now on board with 70 baskets of fish, with a few holes in the belly head. My watch is mending whilst the rest have gone for their tea. All finished on the net as the crew came back from their meal. We went for ours and then watch below beckoned. Called out at midnight with 30 baskets of fish which was all good quality. Hauled again at 0430 hours with about the same. The night sky is going crazy with the Northern Lights. They seem to be dancing to the music being played through the deck loudspeakers!

Finished the fish and breakfast was upon us. I had a nice piece of haddock, hot buster with a cup of char to wash it down. The Mate came off the bridge and said we will be hauling at 0830 hours. Time to take my boots off for an hour and have a cat nap. No sooner had I bobbed off than I was called out to haul the trawl. As usual the doors came up, followed by the dhan lenos, soon after the bobbins and headline cans. All hands pulling together on the trawl and we soon had the wide part in. The net had then been pushed together the in came the winch to make things easier. The cod ends came in with 50 baskets of fish. I was just about to tie the cod line when a voice shouted from the bridge. 'DROP THE DOORS IN - WERE GOING HOME.' which was good news all-round. Doors were brought in with a few lashings on the trawl. The crew then went aft and told the cook that we had finished. His words were that the skipper told him last night. You can't beat a galley radio for all the GOSSIP!!!

After breakfast we went straight into the fish pounds. Everyone's in a good mood whilst we are gutting. We are throwing the hearts and clots at young Ernie, the Deckie Learner, who was taking it all in fun and doing the same to us but its 7 to 1 and he was covered. When we had finished gutting, we sent him off the deck to get cleaned up and showered, whilst we put the deck boards away with the gratings. As the weather was fine, we took the washer down and lashed it against the spare trawl doors, gave the decks a good washdown and the bridge watch went on the bridge. Whilst the men were finishing the fish room, I started to clean the cod ends out and give them a quick once over. I put a few lashes on the trawl then took my wet gear off and popped on the bridge for the morning dram. Whilst dishing it out the mate was sitting in the messdeck and he told me that he would take the afternoon watch and that I would follow him at tea time.

I took the rum back to the bridge, took my boots off, rolled a fag and pulled the ring off a can of beer when Jerry popped his head in my berth and asked for a can. How could I not refuse him? Off he went with a smile on his face. I drank mine then had one more just before lunch which consisted of cow pie, mash with vegetables. I had my fair share and then rolled in. I awoke at 1600 hours, had a nice hot shower and a change of gear. This was my third shower of the trip whilst some hadn't had one at all. Teatime soon arrived. I followed my watch onto the bridge and they had all come clean under the shower. We passed a few ships going north and just before we came off watch we were approaching the Faroe Islands. It only seemed like yesterday that we were alongside in Torshavn.

I came on watch just after breakfast and we've just past Flamborough head. We can now hear the vibration on the ship as we have the tide with us. Finished overhauling the net yesterday morning. All new lashings put on the rail to hang the net on and as soon as we had finished had the ships mats over the side and put down in their places before tea time. The ship has been cleaned all the way through and watchkeepers have done the bridge as well as the chartroom. All brass work is now gleaming, both trainees' [deck and galley] have cleaned the Skipper's berth and he has payed for their bond.

Now approaching the Spurn Light Ship and now on our approach to Grimsby. The Dock Tower standing proudly in the sunshine. A few ships have just passed us near the Bull Light Ship heading towards the fishing grounds as we are now at the end of our trip. We have had our ups and downs but we have made it home where other ships have not. We will never forget those who are no longer with us.

Now in the Lock Gates with a bit of help from the Alfred Bannister (tug). We are now alongside landing quay. The wheel has been put in midships. Telegraph rang to signal finished with engines. I was given a bottle of whisky and sent on my way. I picked my gear up with my fry of fish, climbed on to the fish quay where the wife had been waiting for me. We then got into the car and drove HOME.

The next day went down dock and we turned out 1,800 kits of mostly cod and made £28,000 which was not bad for 20 days. Jerry had to come out of the firm. He didn't get fined although Marconi tried to take him to court and it got thrown out due to provocation. Six months later Jerry came back into the firm.

To be thrown about, up to one's neck in water, hanging on for grim life, not knowing if you will ever see your loved ones again. Coming home from sea and landing in debt and having no mates to help out. On the other hand, coming home with a good catch, making a good trip having plenty of friends, plus hangers on, looking for some easy money, are all parts of the life of a fisherman who have always been hard workers and with fellow fishermen become friends for life!

Andy Jensen took us for another trip but we didn't earn much. We were, fishing East Greenland in March. He could not get to where he wanted to fish because of the ice and we finished fishing at Iceland. The weather was bad and we ended up fishing on Faroe Bank. We made £22,500 with the next two trips averaged £25 000 or so.

14

Boston Concord

The first week in June we sailed again with Billy Balls as skipper. Sailed breakfast time and watches set by lunchtime. We had to be careful in the river with lots of pleasure craft and having weekend sailors in their yachts started to lose all the pleasure craft right up to Whitby. We have had most of the same crew for the last few trips. Bonzo sacked a couple of lads who didn't pull their weight but nobody asked why.

The weather running off had been good. At night times the skies were crystal clear, with shooting stars lightening as they hit the earth's atmosphere. On passing the Faroe Islands we saw puffins and razorbills dipping and diving and, on the surface, their bills filled with sprats. We seemed to have had a harsh winter, so now let's enjoy the summer months. When we had the bond yesterday, we were told that we will be going to Hali Bank and ignoring what other ships were doing.

Passing a few boats on Hari Kari who were finishing off their trips. The next day we passed Largeness then Grimsey. During the evening we were greeted with the Northern Lights skipping across the horizon. We just took it for granted, where people are now paying thousands of pounds with no guarantee that they will be seen. We saw them for free! Pete Bowman is now cook and the food that he does wouldn't be far off your favourite restaurant but still we had the old favourites like a pan of shackles etc. The difference between him and other cooks was that he served your meals on a plate and he soon got to know each person's size meals.

We have now reached Hali Bank and we are about to haul our first tow of the trip. As usual the after door then the fore door came up and then secured. As we were heaving on the bridles the cod ends surfaced and then began to stretch out into the belly and baiting's. We seem to have hit the jackpot with no other ships near us. We emptied the cod ends about six times. It was mostly very large cod with a mixture of large haddocks in between. We were by ourselves for about three days averaging about 70 baskets a haul and no mending.

The next day a vessel appeared over the horizon with the biggest funnel on the Humber, it was the St Dominic. He spoke to the Skipper on the radio and shortly after he was fishing alongside us. The weather has been kind and we have been gutting in our smocks. A few more ships joined us over the course of a week but we have had our fair share of fish. We did a short steam and started fishing at Kempanes where we had a couple of descent days' work.

After ten days we have 2,000 kits in up to now. It has still been hard work but thankfully it has mainly been cleaning fish which hopefully we can get a good market. We finished off fishing at Surtsey/Vestmanyer and ended up with another couple of hundred kits and the order was given to 'DROP THE DOORS IN, WE ARE GOING HOME!'

There are not many trips like this, when you get an easy trip. When we left location, we had in our nets 50 baskets of fish which took about an hour to clean, with the weather being flat of calm. We dropped the washer on the main deck and secured it. We cleaned the cod ends and nets with of old fish before lashing the trawl and chains on the bobbins.

Steaming home we did our watches, overhauled the trawl and its workings, greased all the main blocks up the mast and this was down to me. The ship was cleaned internally and externally. The last meal we had was steak with all the trimmings. After tea the galley was scrubbed ready for docking. Just after breakfast we docked and we all went home to our loved ones.

I went home and at tea time went to my father in laws house with my wife who was heavily pregnant. In the evening we watched football [England v Germany]. During the end of the match her waters broken and she was then taken to the maternity hospital in Cleethorpes. In due course my daughter was born which made me very happy.

I went down dock to landed, had a few beers and went to see my daughter. As I reached the maternity building our Skipper was waiting to visit his daughter who was in the maternity hospital. On seeing me, he told me that he was bringing me out of the Concord and putting his brother-in-law with him. He said; 'It's not what you know, it's who you know!'

This took the happiness away but on the plus side I had a week at home and went back in the Kestrel.

When I came home in the Kestrel, I was asked whether I wanted to go back in the Concord as the Skipper wanted me back my reply was; 'No thank you!'

Random Memory - All Sorts of People

Lots of people came to Grimsby/Hull in the late 60/70s and went to sea in trawlers. There were many different backgrounds such as ex-offenders, merchant navy, coal miners, people running from the law, even lumberjacks.

Lots settled down to the hard graft where they had four meals a day, a bed to sleep in [sometimes]. Many married local girls and settled down in Grimsby/Hull and the surrounding areas. We made lots of new friends, fell out with a few, but that's our way of life.

Remembering all those early winter mornings getting dressed and ready for the early morning tides. Sitting in a taxi, being driven all over town, picking crew members up. Approaching the North Wall often seeing the dock rats which were nearly as big as cats, scurrying about the quayside. Arriving alongside your berth and having to climb up those steep ladders on to the whaleback to join your ship. Do we miss those days and would we do it today? YES - WE WOULD

Oh, and the days that you did at sea with a full hold of fish, with market prices high and walking through your front door. With the children rummaging through your kit bag for all the treats you purchased in the bond. Happy days!

Choosing to go to sea as livelihood, not just for a trawlerman but any seamen, is tough on their family. They miss lots of family occasions, especially watching the children grow up. This is where the wife plays an important role as they are the 'mother and father' whilst their partner is away. They have complete responsibility for the household keeping everything going, so many things, too numerous to mention. Fisherman are a Special Breed but so is A Fisherman's Wife. This goes for All Seafaring Folk!

15

Boston Concord – White Sea

Just been down dock to sign on. Had a £5 sub with a £20 tax rebate. I put my gear onboard but not sailing till early Friday morning. The other Bosuns gear is still on board so I had the watchman roll it up ready for taking off.

Last day at home!

I never liked this day, knowing how difficult it was to leave your family whilst us men folk worked in often harsh weather conditions, but it's a way of life that we chose to do!

I Spent the day visiting the family and getting a few things from the local stores instead of on the North Wall. In the evening played with kids before bedtime and watched a bit of TV. We had an early night having to be up at 0700 hours. Never really had a good night's sleep the night before sailing. Alarm set to go off at 0600 hours. Up, dressed and then downstairs and awaiting taxi.

I said my goodbyes which does not get any easier and climbed into the Taxi.

Here we go AGAIN!!!

Been in a taxi for nearly an hour being driven all over the Grange then on to the Nunny and lastly to Waltham picking up the crew. We finally reach the North Wall and up those steep ladders we go. Health and Safety would have a field day the way we had to join the ships. I reached my cabin and the work gear from the other bosun, with a note attached saying I could have the gear and what's left to let the crew have. I had a quick nosey in the bag and discovered a new duck suit with a pair of white boots being my size. I removed them along with gloves and mittens and the rest I put in the drying room. The person I replaced never went back to sea. In later years he ran the Cons club with his wife Carol. I quickly grabbed a pot of tea and went to the deckies area where I found a couple of new faces from the last time I had been here, along with Tommy Burton the new cook. I was offered a dram which I took and I then a voice shouted; 'Bosun to the Bridge!'

After a few steering alterations, we are now going through the lock gates and away to sea. The Skipper is pleased that I did come back but it might have been a bit different if the Kestrel didn't have to go into dry dock which will be for a couple of weeks or more. People don't realise that when we are in dock and the ship has maintenance we are not on pay, so I had no other choice really. Passing the Burcom and heading for Spurn Lightship. We were making 15 knots of speed. Abeam of the Lightship and the course was set NNE.

Although we have just left dock, I always wanted more time at home.

It's my turn for the first watch and my 2 watchmates soon came on the bridge with one of them bringing me a cuppa. Very heavy traffic near the mouth of the river, with not everyone adhering to rules of the road. Tea time soon approached and I was relieved on the bridge by the Mate. I made my way aft and had a bowl of shackles then flopped into my bunk.

What a difference four days make being at home, snuggled up with the wife and kids. Whereas now just leaving Lodigen Pilot, freezing our bollocks off [so to speak] whilst waiting to pick up the pilots. We had spent a couple of hours overhauling the trawl and changed a couple of bobbins, with a couple of broken Lancaster's (spacers between bobbins). Now pleased that it has all been finished as we are now going through the fjords. The heavy snow is now beginning to freeze. The gratings and pound boards have all been put up and we can relax a bit knowing that we are already to shoot the trawl when the time comes. After lunch it had been my turn for the bridge watch. The two pilots that are on board I have not seen before. They mid-30s in age and very friendly and polite. Both come from fishing backgrounds and understood what kind of profession we are in. The afternoon soon past. I had the deck learner on watch with me whilst the regular watch person had been getting the fish room ready. I had him writing the compass out just from north to east. It is best to learn quadrants first and he seems eager to learn. Teatime came and I was relieved by the mate. I sat down to a mixed grill with all the trimmings. It was the kind of meal that you would gladly pay for ashore. The cook was Tommy Burton and I had the pleasure of sailing with him in previous ships. The meals were always tasty, not like some chefs whose meals were full of grease. After tea I was invited into the messdeck for a couple of hours playing 'Crash' with cards then, 'Dominoes Out'. Just before 2100 hours I retreated to my cabin.

GUTTED, I've left my GARDENING BOOKS at HOME!'

The pilots were put ashore by the pilot boat early morning. As breakfast is nearly upon us, we were all called out to get something to eat before we shoot the net.

Where has all the time gone. It only feels like yesterday we were docking. I discovered that the skipper had a big fallout with the other bosun and that he had sacked him. I'm not getting involved but if it wasn't for the Boston Kestrel being on the slips would I be back here? The answer would be NO! The important thing is I have a family and Mortgage to pay along with bills. 0800 hours went on the deck to prepare the trawl. Most of the net had been frozen solid but with a bit of clouting it with spanners, hammers and other methods the net was now free. Tapped on the bobbin chains which in turn were now free. Both otter boards were put over the rail. secured by chain and hook, checked the cod line had been tie. It would be pointless putting the net over without this option and it has been done a few times lol.

The cod ends hanging over the side and the order came; 'Let go!' which were then dropped into the water. The rest of the net usually follows but this time we put the out hauler (yoyo) into the belly of the trawl to help pull the net which we soon saw it disappear over the side, followed by the bobbins and then the headline. The order came; 'Lower the dhan lenos!' which we did. I took my place on the fore door winch and when the order came lowered the trawl doors. The order then came; 'Pay away!' which on this ship meant putting the winch gear into reverse, the wires into the water, the correct depth was soon reached. We unshipped the clutches on the winch and in turn attached the messenger wire onto the forward warp which when released it put the fore and aft warp into the towing block which were positioned on the starboard quarter. When both were locked into the block the aft gang shouted; 'ALL SQUARE!' Now it was a waiting game until we hauled the NET. Watches are now se. Roll on teatime when I'm watch below.

First haul produced very little fish maybe 20 baskets. We should be hauling again soon but just been notified that a Norwegian Fishery Patrol are boarding us to make sure everything's hunky dory and above board. Three Norwegian Naval crew members came aboard prior to hauling the nets. One person went on the bridge and the others watched from the portside whilst we hauled. The doors came up, the bobbins followed with the headline soon afterwards. At the time it was snowing heavily which didn't help much as soon as the net hit the deck, the naval officers produced triangular shapes which they probed the nets on sizes of meshes. Obviously, we passed with flying colours! I undid the cod line with 50 baskets of cod. They glanced at the fish, had a quick nosey around the fish room, finding nothing untoward and finally a look at the spare nets. All three then congregated on the bridge with their findings. After a short time, they were back onto naval craft. I proceeded to tie the Cod line and to carry on putting the gear back over the side as though it had been another day at the office. Finished shooting the net and was then called to the bridge for a rum issue which went down nicely.

Fishing forty miles off the Cape. We are averaging 50 baskets of good quality fish, mainly Cod with a sprinkling of Haddocks. It's nearly 0130 hour and I'm standing in the fish pounds, gutting away, listening to Johnny Cash 'Walking the Line'. The fish pounds are nearly clear when the warps begin to pull out which means that we have 'come fast' on the Seabed and the ship came to a stop! The winch was started and the order came to knock out, (warps in the towing block) and the order came; 'to heave on the warps!' Slowly we started recovering the Warps when suddenly we were free of the underwater obstruction. The after door appeared covered in thick mud. Minutes later the fore door had been the same. The net soon surfaced without any visible damage. The net came in, cod ends, followed with 20 baskets of fish. Order came to lift the doors out of the water as we were moving a couple of miles to a new position. The skies were giving us a firework display with the Northern Lights in full view. I climbed over the gratings and was back gutting the fish. We managed to clear the fish and grabbed a quick cuppa before we shot the nets away again.

Nets back over and All Square Aft! Time to grab an hour of Gash Sleep!

DISCOVERED that we have a ships 'RAT' onboard, tittle tattling to the BRIDGE. It's good to feed these types of people with false information!!!

The fishing has taken off at the Cape grounds but there are good reports coming from BEAR ISLAND.

Trawl Doors are dropped in and the bit of fish from last haul is now being cleaned. Trawls lashed up to the rail without any damage. Full Steam Ahead. We will be steaming for about 30 hours.

After nearly 30 hours we have finally reached our destination, Bear Island. Looking around the horizon we are not by ourselves, with may be 20 ships, mostly from the Humber ports, with a couple of Soviets (old coal burners). It's nearly lunchtime and I was told to call all hands out, minus those on watch below. Tucked in to a big bowl of stew and dumplings. Proper rib clinging food. Only had one bowl full as we have to put the net over soon. Just after 1300 hours through the tannoid system came the order, 'Shooto!' With waterproofs on we went on the deck and it was bloody freezing. I was pleased I had a couple of layers of clothes on, including long johns, jumper and smock.

Firstly, we undid the lashings on the trawl with a few chains included. Secondly the after door was put over the rail quickly, followed by the fore door. Approximately 30 minutes later the trawl had been deployed and all square was called. Before we left the deck, we made sure the scupper doors were all closed in preparation before we hauled in a couple of hours. I was called to the bridge to take a rum issue which we haven't had for a couple of days. I took the remainder of the rum bottle back to the bridge. The Skipper told me to get my feet up as he would be taking the first tow. After 3 hours we hauled with 50 baskets of spraggy codlings, we caught bigger fish when I had been here before. Teatime soon approached and was now ready for my tea.

Called out at midnight. We had 200 baskets of fish with both trawls split. It going to be a busy night and to make matters worse it's snowing quite heavily. By 0300 hours we managed to get a trawl ready and we shot it away. The spare trawl on the port side both myself and the mate stood mending it whilst the lads gutted the fish. Luckily all the net was there but it just had a large split in the belly and baiting's with a smaller hole in the forward top wing. Happy days - cold wet and miserable. Don't think that in today's society anyone would put up with the conditions that we worked in 45/50 years ago!

Fishing has been good averaging 50 baskets which is a steady living. It's done nothing but snow which sometimes seemed like blizzard conditions, as the wind swept across the decks. We are now 12 days away and we are doing quite well with 900 kits. We keep feeding the messdeck rat false information. How sad when people start running up and down the bridge. Just after breakfast the snow cleared up with visibility up to 10 miles or more. We are all stood in the fish pounds gutting the fish and just over the rail we saw a Russian trawler quite close to us coming up our starboard side towing faster than us, when suddenly are warps began to pull out. We have come fast or so it seemed. The Russian trawler had become dog tied with us (picked up are net).

The Skipper shouted to knockout the warps and we began to heave on the nets. The order came to stop heaving, then told to lower the warps in the water. The Russian skipper would take our net on their deck and untangle our gear which he did. We were quite close to the Russian ship and we could see a person on the other ships whaleback with what looked like a gun. We were later told it had been a person making sure that the crew didn't try to get on board our ship. Just before lunch we were told to start heaving on our trawl. Within 15minutes our net was on the deck without a mesh broken. We shot the net back over soon afterwards. The morning rum issue was taken round with the skipper being in a good mood after the morning's episode. Tea time soon came and went. My watch lashed the spare trawl on the portside to the ships rail which was the first chance that we have had since changing the trawl. We hauled the trawl mid-afternoon with 50 baskets of sprags.

We've been averaging 50 baskets of spraggy coddling Each haul with a splashing of haddocks. Towing for 4 hours and having a decent catch each haul. We had one mishap during the night when we parted a headline wire and it had been an easy fix. The deckie learner came up to me nearly crying and I asked what was the matter. One of our deckhands had been teaching him to play cribbage with cards but now they had started to play for money which he didn't have, but he said he could give him the money from his share in dock. I flew into a rage with the person who had been teaching the deckie learner and told him, in a few words, not to ask for the money. He said he did not agree and that the deckie learner 'Had got to learn!!' So, I smacked him one and said; 'So do you! You're not teaching someone and taking money from him!' Never heard any more from him.

We have heard that they are having a tough time at Iceland. They want us out of their waters and to reduce quotas. Some ships have had their gear chopped out! Our government has sent our Royal Navy with Deepwater Tugs to protect our ships. We will be going home tomorrow. We have 1,600 kits of fish on board with 24 hours more fishing time. It's now teatime with cow pie, mash and vegetable followed by treacle duff and custard. The weather is very calm with the snow now turning to rain which means it is getting warmer.

There are no better words heard at sea than; 'Drop the doors in. Lash her up. We're going HOME!'

When we dock, we will be 22 days, dock to dock. This last haul we had 50 baskets of fish. Half the belly of the net has gone but we will try and get this fixed before we dock. We have 1,600 miles to go before we dock and we should average 14 knots, with a bit in hand. The weather is not in our favour and the ship has eased in to slow speed whilst we are gutting on the deck. Bits of spray are coming off the whaleback with salt water hitting our eyes and trickling down our necks. It's nearly 0500 hours when we finished on the deck. We secured everything on the deck as there is nothing worse than being called out to secure loose objects on the deck. The mate sang out on the tannoid system for me to relieve him at 0730 hours when the steaming watches are set. I had a nice fish sarnie with a mug of tea.

Soon afterwards I went on the bridge and took charge of the watch. I looked at both of my watchmates and what a sorry sight. Both of them looked tired out and physically drained. I should imagine that I looked the same to them. The Skipper rolled out at 0900 hours and asked for a cup of tea which soon arrived from my watchmate. He commented that the crew had worked well together and the mate's fish tally would be 1,700 kits. Just before lunch I took the rum round to those that were up and soon after I was relieved for my meal which was cow pie without the horns, mashed potatoes, tinned carrots and peas, with a thick onion gravy which was just like granny used to make. I stumbled into my cabin and had a quick smoke. I took my socks off then rolled in with my Norwegian gardening magazines. With the purr of the engines and the steady rolling of the ship, I soon went into a deep slumber. The next thing I remember was the galley boy shouting me for tea which I had followed by a long shower and a change of clothes which made me feel like the living after some rest and a decent nap. Now looking forward to some home time with my FAMILY.

Finally, we docked last night about teatime. The wife met me in and her auntie, who lived next door to us baby sat the children whilst I got home. I took a fry of fish off the ship along with tobacco and cigarettes. People don't realise how lucky we are. We come home after a three-week trip to find the house is all clean and tidy. More so having plenty food in the cupboards. Then to climb into bed with fresh laundry.

After a good night's sleep, it was then time to get up and dressed, go out and get my haircut at Billy Raymond's with a friendly chat to follow. Soon after I went on the dock to find we had turned out 1,950 kits of fish and made £31,000.

I met the wife near the bank and deposited my settlings and kept a bit a side for treats and of course a few beers which I had after going into the White Knight, then on to Billy Cairns before having a fish and chip dinner at the Pea Bung which was always a nice meal, in the 70s as it is today!

Time ashore seems to go by so quickly and we've been told to go to Iceland next trip to give support to the rest of the fleet.

16

Boston Concord – Iceland

It doesn't seem five minutes since we docked and now it's time to go away again. Its nearly 0130 hours and I'm up and dressed. I went to bed at tea time just to try and get a couple of hours kip which didn't help as my head kept spinning about our next trip. Although I enjoyed the long soak in the bath with Raydox crystals it's going to be a while before I have another bath as we do have showers on the ship which is not the same. Just having a nice cup of tea with bottled milk, as on the ships we have evaporated milk in tins. Most times at sea I have my drinks without any milk. I just heard a car outside - is it my taxi? A quick look out of the window and I discover it is not. I have a few more cigarettes and then I hear a knock on the door. The time had come for me to go but before I leave, I kiss the kids and the wife and tell them that I love them. Then it IS time to pick up my kitbag, close the front door. I'm now inside the Taxi and heading down dock to join the ship.

Sailed at 0400 hours and it seemed like ages waiting to go away. We had one crew member who went missing from his home address and he made his own way down dock an hour after we all had arrived. As soon as he stepped aboard the mooring ropes were thrown off the quay and the boarding ladder was then stored into position. We were eventually out of the dock, up to the Spurn Lightship with the course set for North half West. The Mate took the first watch with me going on at teatime which gave me chance to catch up on some sleep. Off the bridge for a quick pot of tea with a sarnie, then to my cabin. Most of my gear had been put away and eventually I turned in.

Called out just before tea for watcho and feeling refreshed. I had a bite to eat which was bacon, eggs, sausages and chips. Simple food for sailing day but very nice as well. I made my way up to the bridge with my two watchmates who were Big Jerry, who came back with us and Johnny Chase. We relieved the watch and settled down for the night. Reports are coming in on the big set (radio) that the gunboats are causing havoc on the fishing grounds by harassing the fishing boats and are now chopping the warps (towing wires). I just hope that we can get a trip in and let the powers that be sort it out. All we want is to earn a living. Fishing has always been a dangerous job, just to put fish on to the table.

Weather is nearly flat of calm with visibility about 20 miles. We are leaving the land and all we see in the distance is the loom of the land with lighthouses giving off flashing lights. The night time sky is crystal clear with the stars sparkling away and the occasional shooting star flying across the sky, leaving a trail until it disappears. We had our idle chit-chat to pass the watch away with background music which was usually radio Luxembourg. Soon the watch came to an end and the Mate's watch relieved us. We then made our way aft hoping once more that we get a good sleep. I opened my cabin door and to my surprise there on my seat locker were a dozen or so magazines with ladies of the night, displaying flower arranging.

I did the early morning watch. I went below and just before tea we put the net over the side. We are at 'Workingman's Bank'. The Skipper called me and the Mate on to the bridge telling us to have the crew in readiness as there are gunboats creeping up on the ships and cutting the warps. After being told I left the bridge and told the lads who were not very happy but they knew the score before we sailed. We hauled at about 2000 hours with 30 baskets of fish. My watch was called out at midnight for hauling time. When it was time I went on the deck, looking around the horizon there must have been about 40 ships in the area.

I later discovered that we had a few deep-water tugs including The Statesman which is a hospital ship, The Miranda and a Royal Naval presence looking after us. There had been a few ships that have had their warps cut by the Icelandic gunboats Tyr, Eagar and Thor. What the ships are doing now is having to take it in turns putting their nets over whilst another ship followed over their gear preventing the cutting of the warps. Most ships are working on the 'kidney bank' or around the 'telegraph' areas. If you can get a two-hour tow in, the ships are averaging 50 baskets. As soon as anybody sees the gunboats the Naval craft, together with the tugs, go to try and head them off. We did this for about a week and we had 800 kit of fish in.

I rolled out just after midnight just laid in the water, when I turned to. The skipper came to my cabin and asked; 'Am I with the rest of the crew?' Having just woken up, I didn't know what had happened. Apparently, the 'messdeck lawyer' had got the crew to refuse to fish at Iceland with what's going on. The Skipper said; 'We will fish at the Faroes' but in both messdecks it stated on the ships contract 'Deep-Water Areas'. I told the skipper; 'I'm not involved in this!' I then went into the mess and you've guessed it. The 'messdeck lawyer' had a smirk on his face thinking he had done well.

I was then ordered onto the bridge where the Skipper asked; 'What are the crew doing?' and I told him that they were still refusing to work. I was then ordered to drop the doors in, lash the trawl in, 'We're going home!'.

I have never felt so low at sea when a minority of the crew could do this.

Three days later I arrived home and surprised the wife. 'What are you doing home so early?' I told her myself what had happened and she then gave me a letter. It read that I and the rest of the crew had to go before the 'kangaroo court' (Trawler Owners) to see if the crew were going to be suspended from going to sea.

The next day, as instructed, I went down dock and was told by the ships husband that the 'kangaroo court' didn't want to see us and no further action would be taken. I was just about to leave the office when I was called into the runner's place. He advised me that we are sailing in three days' time and that BONZO would be taking us. He also said that most of the crew had been changed and may I add in my opinion, for the better!

True to form we sailed again early morning and was told to look in both messdecks. The Ships Contract had been altered and now stated - **ALL AREAS could be FISHED.**

17

Boston Concord – Iceland

Another dreaded morning time for sailing. I'm not complaining because it's the life I chose. Having a young family, it's always a burden getting up early morning and waiting for that dreaded knock which came at 0600 hours. I put my gear in the taxi, went back inside and up the stairs to kiss both the kids and then the wife with a quick cuddle. It's off down the stairs, out the front door to take my place in the car. I just sat there motionless, not wanting to speak, other than good morning but coming home is a different story.

Arrived on the dock, out the taxi and up the ladders with my gear in hand towards my cabin. I quickly put my things away and I went to the crew's area where I found some new faces onboard but some who I knew from different ships. I was offered a quick dram which I was about to neck when a voice over my shoulder said; 'Just the one - we are sailing soon!' It was the new Skipper Bonzo. I sailed with him many times and we both had respect for each other. He had gone around to each cabin saying if you're not happy where we are sailing to then get off the ship. Not one person said a dickybird! Within the next hour we sailed and then the watches were SET.

I've always found it quite heart-breaking at times and feel guilty when I join a ship because I'm leaving my loved ones behind. Its only later in life that you realise and reflect on what your wife or partner did. We were the bread winners but it was the wives, the housekeepers', the mothers of our children, who kept the household going whilst we were away. Not knowing when we went to sea whether we would ever return home again. I'm afraid that in our profession lots of fishermen never returned. It was the time when we were at sea that we can reflect on these thoughts.

I had the first watch and it's now after 0900 hours. We will be off watch at lunch time. I never liked the first afternoon watch with a six hour watch it always seemed endless. Had been chatting away to the Skipper about his intentions and he just stated we would have to face the challenges during the trip. The weather is fine and as we are going down the coastline, we can see fire stacks on the shore line smoking away. As we lose the shore line, we can just make out Hornsea and Easington, with Flamborough Head in the distance, with its chalky cliffs glistening in the sunshine. Lunch time soon approached and the Mate Ken relieved me. We were nearly abeam of Flamborough. My watch, once relieved, made our way to the galley area and took in a quick bite to eat. I then made my way to my cabin for some shuteye. Let's hope that we can catch some fish with what's happening with the gunboats. Time will tell!

The last couple of watches soon passed. This morning we have passed through the Pentland Firth. The weather is practically calm but travelling through the Firth you soon see the tide rips like a giant washing machine, churning up the waters. Plenty of ships have perished running through these areas. We have always closed all the water tight doors with no working on the decks until we pass through.

After lunch I spent a couple of hours on the deck doing one or two modifications to the trawl and adjusted to how the Skipper wanted the bobbins rigged. As soon as we finished, I left the deck and left the finishing touches to the daymen. Before tea I had a hot shower and a change of gear. I washed my clothes in the sit up bath, rinsed them and hung them on a line in the bathroom until they dried. Teatime approached and as I sat eating my tea with the Skipper and Radio Operator, they were talking about how things were going on the fishing grounds which wasn't good news. Plenty of ships have had one or two of their warps chopped by the gunboats. Ships have been told to keep in groups so that our Frigates and Ocean Tugs can protect the majority of them. I had my tea and then went into my cabin for a quick nap before watcho. The Cook did well and serve lamb chops, mash, carrots, cabbage, mint sauce, with a thick gravy. For afters he served spotted dick and custard. If you had a decent chef life was so much better and you had good meals. Now its lights out until later.

Now nearing the fishing grounds and we have been informed we can stay with the Southerly group of trawlers or with the Northern group. The Skipper decided we are going North and just after lunchtime we passed Largeness, with a few local ships going about their business. As we neared them, we could see that they were raising their fists at us and making gestures with their hands. We just carried on ignoring them and we soon approached Grimsey. The watch below was set. Teatime came which consisted of roast beef, Yorkshire puddings, roast potatoes, cabbage, carrots with a thick onion gravy, followed by treacle duff. I consumed my fair share and I rolled down the alleyway into my cabin where sleep soon beckoned me. I was awoken about 0800 hours to the sound of the bobbins going over the side. I better get some more shuteye, with not knowing what lies ahead of this voyage.

After waking up at 2000 hours I couldn't really get back to sleep as I was constantly tossing and turning, as my mind wandered everywhere. I decided to get up and have a shower with a change of gear. I am now feeling refreshed and looking forward to the evening events. Just after 2330 hours the crew were hauling for the first time this trip. I beat the engineers to the porthole and it looks like a decent haul of fish of about 50 baskets.

My watch mates were called at midnight and at 1215 we heard the shout from the aft of 'ALL SQUARE!' On the deck from 1230 until about 0200 hours when the last fish went down the fish room. This was good going as about 50 baskets of fish put away. Took gear off and had a quick cuppa then had an hour on the seat locker or so it seemed. Suddenly I heard them knocking out the block and the watch burst in my cabin saying that 2 gunboats were near us. I took my position behind the winch looking and counting the warp marks. We had 200 fathoms of warp out and we are now down to our last 50. Soon the doors and net came on board with 40 baskets of fish. I was told to get the fish gutted and down the fish room and to see what is happening. The two gunboats steamed through the ships with no reports of having their warps cut. Calm before the storm I'm afraid. Our naval boats, along with the tugs, were shadowing there every move.

0500 hours we put the net back over the side. The weather was now beginning to freshen up. The cook gave the ones that were awake an early breakfast which had gone down nicely with fresh buster and a full English breakfast.

We have had three days fishing without any incident. We have a good presence of Frigates and Ocean-Going Tugs in attendance. The ships fishing in the southern areas are having a sticky time. Ships have had either one warp or both chopped which is a very big risk to life as the tension on the warps, when cut, is like a coiled spring. When cut the tension returns on to the decks of the trawlers. When the

Icelandic's are spotted the tune of, 'Mouldy Old Dough' comes over the VHF radios.

After nearly a week of fishing we have 800 kits on board. When the Everton which was fishing by herself, took a shell just above the waterline, things were beginning to get serious. The gunboats were cutting more warps when working in packs. The ships then had one ship fishing whilst one kept on the stern covering the warps. The Frigates started ramming the Icelandic's to keep them away from our trawlers.

Our government was having talks with the Icelanders to try trying to come to an agreement suitable for both sides but were getting nowhere.

The Icelanders began talk with the Americans' regarding the Air Base that they had on Keflavik. This was a strategic Air Base. Overnight our ships were told to leave the Icelandic waters.

We travelled south fishing around Faroe Bank then later the Shetland Isles waters. After a couple of days, we had our orders for docking. The cry from the bridge had been; **DROP THE DOORS, WE ARE GOING HOME!'**

After dropping the trawl doors in usually everyone's happy but not so on this occasion. Our trip has been cut short and we will be 15 days dock to dock. With most of us all having the same questions running through our minds:

'Will this be the last time we fish Iceland! Will other countries follow suit and throw us out of their waters?

'Will the negotiations restart?'

'I'm only 27 - what will I do if fishing completely stops?'

I took my watch on the bridge. The Skipper and the Radio Operator were saying what we all thought. We had reported 1,000 kits of fish. Most ships had very little in their holds. Finally, we docked and it had been around lunchtime. The ships runner met us in and we asked in unison;

'Are we sailing again and do we have to take our gear off the ship?'

His reply was that he shrugged his shoulders and said; 'I know as much as you!' We should find out tomorrow.

We landed the next day and made £19,000. I didn't bother going for a pint and went home wandering if this was the last time, I would ever go deep water fishing!

18

Boston Concord – Flemish Cap

After a couple of days at home I had been called to the office. There I was told that both the Boston Concord and the Boston Comanche were going to the Flemish Cap, as well as the Labrador coast.

Before we could go across 'the pond', we had to learn how to use the LORAN C which was a newish form of Chart NAVIGATION. Both crews spent a couple of days learning the new method so we could sail. I went upstairs to see the cashier and he gave me a £20 tax rebate. I had a couple of pints in the Clee Park then went home and told the wife the good news.

Later in the day I visited the father-in-law Bill Ferrand, who had been Skipper of the Defiance and Northern Queen. When I told him where we were sailing, he just looked at me and said; 'It's the wrong time of the year to be going there.'

Well, I thought, we will soon find out for ourselves because we are sailing Tuesday. Also, I've just been given a brand new DOPPER [if people can still remember them] and I am taking my moleskin fearnaughts as well!

Up at the crack of dawn ordered for 1000 hours which was a nice change from silly hours. Taxi duly came at 1030 hours. I said my goodbyes to the wife and kids. It's getting harder and harder leaving the wife and kids but bills have to be paid. Ships are still running to the coast but we imagine that the Norwegians and the Russians will put silly limits on the grounds, meaning that fishing will be a thing of the past.

I just feel lucky that I have work and am trying to earn a living. Arrived on the North Wall, clambered out of the taxi up the ladders and made my way aft. I put my gear away whilst I had chance. I went ashore to Coleridge's, to pick up this month's Gardening Magazines, picked a few more items such as gutting gloves and a new venturer gutting knife which I will put somewhere behind the winch to weather up for use.

Back aboard the ship a few new faces once more but they seemed friendly enough. I had learnt how to weigh up people after 24 hours, especially the bullshitters. The 'messdeck lawyer' has gone, Big Jerry is back and has asked to come on watch with me again. You don't argue with the man and I just said; 'Of course you can.' I have sailed with him plenty of times whilst I was a deckie and later as bosun and have never had any problems with him but I know not to wind him up. I am now back on the ship and just passing the bridge when I was told to put my stores in my cabin and to come on to the bridge for sailing. I climbed up the bridge stairs and on to the bridge and exchanged pleasantries with Bonzo. I took hold of the steering gear and as directed used the various courses until eventually we had left the quay and was now outside the docks making our way up the river Humber and on to a new chapter in my life!

Just after midnight and we were abeam of Aberdeen with the harbour lights flashing in the distance. Plenty of shipping plying their trade which were mostly supply boats with a few trawlers heading for the mornings market. Next point of land before we alter course will be Rattary Point which we can just make out tight on the port bow. The Northern Lights are trying to make a display but conditions are not right at this time. We went off watch at 0300 hours and I had a quick sarnie before going below and lunch time soon arrived. I have had a good watch below and feeling refreshed.

At 1300 hours we passed Duncansby Head. Informed the watch to get the dayman to close all the watertight doors prior to going through the Pentland Firth. Instead of passing through and heading towards the Old Man of Hoy we hugged the Northern Coastline going through the short cut known as St Johns Crossing, Thurso Bay and then Dunnet Head. Most of the crew where apprehensive saying are we doing the right thing going to the Flemish Cap but in my opinion it's just another challenge for us. Looking at the coastline we have past John O'Groats were people used to elope without their parents' consent to get married. Teatime soon approached which was Mince pie, mash, carrots, cabbage and gravy followed by sago pudding and jam which is not everyone's favourite but not complaining Sleep soon followed after a few chapters of my reading book, Sven Hazzell Blitzkrieg.

Having just rolled in I had been called out to make up a card school. The game we were playing is called 'rummy' and we are only playing for fun, as I've seen too many arguments over money. Tommy Burton, the cook sat in, Johnny with Micky H and myself had a couple of hours playing cards. Just before 2300 hours I turned in again. When I went on watch at 0300 hours, we are just crossing Loch Erbil. I have been in there a few times as it is a good shelter during gales. We were soon abeam of Cape Wrath, crossing the Minch which when entering took you to places like Ullapool and the Inner Hebrides and Islands such as Skye. Tonight's sky had been full of stars with the phosphorus in the water astern of us being churned by our propellors which gave us an array of light and dark greens shining in our wake, astern of us. The Northern Lights didn't offer much of a display just appearing for a short period of time and as quick as they appeared they had vanished.

We can see the But of Lewis ahead of us with Stornoway not being too far away. I can remember going into there on a Sunday hoping to get a pint or two with engine failure but the law stated that the islanders did not open on the Sabbath. I don't know if the law has changed but if it hasn't don't go there on a Sunday! As we are crossing the water the wind is beginning to pick up from the Southeast which is just aft of our beam. With a gentle rolling of the ship will hopefully rock me to sleep when we go below. 0700 hours watches were called, as well as the daymen. When relieved from my watch I asked the mate if he needed me on deck but he replied that he didn't. I took my place in the crews messdeck to eat a hearty breakfast. I turned in and with the rolling motion of the ship I was soon sound asleep. I slept like a log and was called out mid-afternoon for my Bond.

I had from breakfast to teatime off and so I took time-out for a shower, played cribbage with the cook for an hour or so but now I'm back on watch feeling refreshed. We are just coming up to the Flanner Islands in the Outer Hebrides. This is where three lighthouse keepers went missing in the nineteen hundreds I believe and now there is a film about it. I can't remember whether the islands were called 'the seven brothers or sisters. I'm sure that someone will know. We are now coming to the end of using the Decca Navigator but I have been comparing positions with the Loran C and feel happy using this new system. The Deckie Learner came on watch for an hour with us and he started to recite the compass to us. He seems to be getting the hang of it now. I can remember many a fisherman had a compass rose tattooed on their hand so that they could understand which course to steer. Little George, the Deckie Learner, also started to splice soft rope for now. I don't mind teaching anyone if only they want to learn. Those that say that they already know, to me are a waste of space.

The weather's not too bad, still south easterly but now a gentle breeze. The next piece of land we might see will be Rockall which is a single Rock sticking out of the sea which the French say belongs to them. I've been fishing there a few times and not saying that they are small fish but they were all born yesterday! Certain areas you can catch decent size haddocks. Some of the fish we called rounders and we threw them straight into the washer, un-gutted, losing a few pounds only for each Kitt. Well, the watch has passed by quickly. The Northern lights are now making a show, with every appearance they flutter across the evening sky giving us a free viewing. At 2300 hours I handed over the watch. I am well pleased with using the new navigation system and I can now go below pleased with myself. I had a quick cup of hot chocolate in which I took it to my cabin, where I sat down with a smoke before I retired for the evening. Do I get the gardening books out or the war books? In the end I decided neither. I turned my bunk light out and with a gentle movement of the ship I quickly went to sleep.

This time tomorrow we should be on the fishing grounds. I have kept busy making a new trawl, with cod ends which means that we now have three trawls complete with enough gear, in parts, maybe to make another one. Night times past either playing cards or draughts. I tried my hand at chess but I can't seem to get the hang of this. Mind you, going home I may attempt trying once more. I have just had a full English breakfast thanks to the cook! I am now off to get some shuteye!

Seems monotonous; on-watch, off-watch, works all done on deck. I came on watch at teatime and you could now feel the outside temperatures beginning to fall plus we have seen quite a bit of snow as well. The weather has been kind but at times we come up against some Atlantic rollers when the seas become unsteady. It's like being on a big dipper, going up then down again. Just one after the other of large swells of sea. We must be nearing land as we have seen a few gulls appearing now and again. You may not see any for a while but as soon as the waste bin goes over the side magically the gulls appear. It's like opening a can of beer in your cabin then someone's standing by your door saying are we having one.

The crew seem quite happy coming to sea but we don't have much choice if we need work. Of course, we all moan that's only natural. We keep hearing static on the VHF Radio with the occasional words being spoken but as of this time we can't make out any words. During the day we came across a pod of Orcas swimming tirelessly in the distance oblivious to us. We have now lost nearly all the British radio stations, including Luxembourg. We are now listening to chewing grass and saddle music. Just hoping that we can find some decent fish and make a living. I have every confidence in Bonzo and who is going to argue with him? Not me, for one ha-ha!

Well, we have finally arrived at our destination just after breakfast. I had been called out with the rest of the crew and left the Mate and his two watchmates in their bunks as we have now started watch belows. I had a nice brekkie with porridge followed by a piece of smoked fish, washed down with a mug of tea. Just after 0800 hours I ventured on the deck. Thick fog greeted us with a mixture of snow and ice. The ship eased in with her speed with the command coming from the bridge that we could start to put the gear over the side. Firstly, we put the otter boards over (trawl doors) the sides whilst crew members unlashed the trawl from its lashings tied on the ships rail, the chains were taken off the bobbins and I then made my way to the cod ends to tie the cod line. I sang up to the bridge telling them that we were ready and the reply came 'to chuck the net over!'

The cod ends went out on the yo-yo with the yo-yo hook put into the belly. The net began to pull away from the ships side. The bobbins and rubber weights went over soon, followed by the headline float. Dhan lenos gently lowered down, followed by the trawl doors. The ship began to make speed, then the command came to pay away the warps. On this ship we reversed the winch, shipped into the winch clutches. The noise she made sounded like a tank but the benefits we had were huge plus we were under cover as well. Soon the depth of water had been reached, winch unshipped from the gear then the messenger hook put on the forward warp which in turn collected the after warp which was then contained into the towing block. The order came from aft 'ALL SQUARE!' Before we left the deck, we checked that all the scupper doors were now closed.

We have dense fog and icing which chills you to the bone. The nets have been broken with a few large holes which makes mending a lot harder to do. I've known of people peeing on their hands to keep them warm. We are only averaging about 30 baskets for 3-hour tows. We have just repaired the net once more and put the net back over. We had a quick smoke then onto the deck to clean the fish which felt like cutting cardboard, so to speak. Just as we had finished, the fog lifted and we sighted a few trawlers. There were a couple of large Russian factory ships with German university class type stern draggers. There are a few areas closed to us due to long liners, mainly Faroese. A couple of Portuguese boats are here with us which look like coasting vessels which carry a few dory boats which are put over the side with a few days' food with either one or two persons in each boat. After a couple of days, the fish is taken off them and they are supplied with stores. Lots of these types of boats have been lost at sea.

We have just come dog tied with an effing Russian trawler. We are in a wide area to fish and then this happens. We had been towing for nearly 3 hours when the ship came astern of us, shot his net and picked up our net. Weather is calm and our trawl is now on his deck and they are trying to untangle the trawl doors. The ship is about 200 feet from us and we are getting commands to pay more warp away. When told to do so, taking it in turns with the Mate behind the winch whilst the rest of the lads keep warm with hot drinks. We keep seeing what looks like a person on their foredeck who looks like he has a rifle in his hands. Hoping we don't get shot but we have been informed it is in case anyone tries to get over to our ship. We can now see that they are using burning gear but it soon becomes apparent that they are using it on their gear.

After a couple of hours, we were told to start heaving on our gear. I was pleased that it had been my turn to go aft to warm up. I made it back on deck just as the after door came up. It was all battered but intact. It was quickly followed by the fore door which looked ok. The Skipper took a turn out of her on the bridles then the command came to start hauling which we did and to our amazement the trawl came up complete with about 40 baskets of fish. The net went over again and an issue of rum came around on deck with the mate telling us that after the next haul we are going to a fishing bank called Rittur to try our luck there with the

Comanche, who is already there catching more than us. Just after lunch we dropped the trawl in, lifted the doors inboard then started steaming. Little did we know what would happen NEXT!

We have been steaming now for a few hours, with just a slight spray which is coming aboard and freezing instantly. The snow is pelting down and it is getting difficult to look out of the bridge windows but luckily, we have two revolving windows both fitted with heaters which allows us to see through them. The sea has started to freeze which looks like paw prints on the sea which are now beginning to join up together. A few icebergs have been reported in our area but we have not seen any ourselves. The Chief has been up on the bridge saying the temperatures are getting higher, believing that the water intakes are beginning to freeze up. We have now come clear of the pancake ice and we should be fishing either before or after break time. The snow has eased and we don't seem to be making any more ice which is a good thing. Teatime arrived with the choice tonight being fish and chips or cowpie with mash peas and gravy. I chose the latter.

After my tea I had a quick smoke and then turned in for the night. About 2130 hours I woke up to the fire alarm going off. Waking from a deep sleep to being fully alert. I opened my cabin door with my life jacket and dressed in warm clothing. I was told that the fire was at the top of the engine room which was the domestic boiler and that the engineers were working on it to put it out which they successfully achieved. One of the deckies opened the engine room door and the lagging around the pipes ignited again. I was told to prevent people from opening the door of the engine room again, as it was nearly sorted. After about 5 minutes the fire was out. It is your worst NIGHTMARE having a fire on board a ship or anywhere to be truthful. I helped the engineers to refill the extinguishers followed by a nice cuppa and then back to sleep.

I awoke just before brekkie and had a cup of tea or two with a few smokes. After breakfast ventured on the deck to get things ready for shooting the nets. To our surprise the net had not frozen solid and within 30 minutes we were back inside the accommodation. We are now on Rittur Bank. We hauled just before lunch with 200 baskets of fish which were mainly Squaddies (red bream). They are back breaking fish although we didn't need to gut them but they had large spikes on their backs which often caught you unawares. I was called onto the bridge to send a nogging around. Just after lunch another 200 baskets of squaddies. It's alright putting them down the fish room but they don't make much money. We lifted the trawl doors and started steaming Northerly and we passed a few ships which were a lot bigger than us, going Southerly. What do they know that we don't? Well, we will soon find out WHY!

We have had 2 days fishing, catching an average of 40 baskets of cod and more squaddies. The Chief went on the bridge with an engine room job. We are at this time. just outside of St Johns harbour. We have been told to get the inner and outer lights in transit which will take us into port. As we have now entered, we are directed to our berth on the quayside. We have just tied up and have been given a courtesy flag to put up. The bond locker has been sealed and the Immigration Officers interview all crew members. Those without a passport or discharge book are not allowed ashore. I asked the Skipper for permission to go ashore and he just waived me off, saying; 'As long as you're not by yourself!' About three of our crew climbed over the spare doors on the portside to get off the ship and once off we made our way into the shopping area. We were just about to cross the road when a whistle was blown. There, facing us was a Mountie with a trudgen in his hand. He told us to cross on the zebra crossing or we would be lifted for 'jay walking'. Welcome to Newfoundland!

Enjoyed my stroll around St Johns harbour where there were lots of cafes and restaurants. We went back to the ship after a couple of hours. The Skipper had been invited ashore with the Mate and I was told to stay on board to look after things as we had bond on board. Teatime approached with a nice mixed grill with all the trimmings. I duly thanked the cook for a lovely meal and took my place on the bridge. Looking out of the bridge window I noticed what looked like a coaster when in fact it had been a Portuguese mother ship that carried the dory boats, which were taken in and out of the sea. Apparently, it had been in a few hours. The deckie learner (Eric) came onto the bridge to learn about the compass and rope splicing which he held in his hand. He was very keen and willing to learn. I was just showing him how to do an eye splice, when I noticed what looked like a riot van pulling up to the Portuguese coaster. It then opened the back doors and started hurling bodies onto the quayside. They had apparently all been drinking and instead of arresting them, they man handled the persons and took them out of the way back to ship. I popped down below and gave the crew the info on the Mounted Police.

The Skipper came back just before 2100 hours and told me I could go ashore, giving me 20 dollars. I quickly showered putting on clean clothes and I was ready for the town. A couple of us went together including Ernie and the Mate, making sure we crossed the road on the zebra crossing, this time. We found a local pub with country music blasting out.

Within an hour we came across a night club/bar, called the 'PORTHOLE', where we paid an entrance fee of a couple of dollars to the door staff and was told not to cause any trouble. 'Who Us? The door staff told us on the QT that crews left their watches with them for 20 dollars, then the next day they returned to pay for the watches return. We left there just after midnight without any incidents. I woke up just before breakfast with the news that we would be spending another day and night in dock.

Not much happening on the ship and was sitting in my cabin when a knock on the door took my attention. I opened the door to find the Skipper standing there, smiling saying that there were two strangers that I would be interested in talking to. I discovered that they were both Jehovah's Witnesses. I listened to their banter and bid them farewell. I quickly made my way to the bridge were Bonzo just smirked at me.

Teatime soon came upon us and I was asked whether I was going ashore. I just said; 'No, I'm skint!' The cook asked if I wanted to trade his watch in to go ashore and I accepted his offer. We had a good night ashore, using the cooks watch as collateral. Just after breakfast I was called out for sailing. We still had two men ashore from last night. They were given until 0900 hours but they were nowhere to be seen and we sailed. About an hour after we sailed, we were told to return to port to pick up the two men and the Fisheries Inspector who wanted to inspect the fish hold. Bonzo refused to answer the call. We were now on the way home. I went aft when we left St Johns and bumped into the cook on the way down. He just shrugged his shoulders laughing at me. Should I ask him what time it is?

We are nearly midway across the Atlantic Ocean heading home. The first eighteen hours from St Johns we kept getting demands from the Canadian Fisheries to return to port which we ignored. On the Mates watch he had the Coastguard airplane fly past and once again they were ignored. We have come through a couple of ice fields without any worries. Now on the third day and the weather is westerly 8/9. Mid-morning, I was just about to take an issue of rum around to those that were out, when we felt the stern lift, by a following sea, which in turn began to swamp the decks. Instinctively I eased the speed down and the engineers responded immediately. The ship eased down and the decks soon cleared of water. We are now running at 3/4 speed and doing 15 knots. The rum was then issued without further incidents.

The atmosphere aboard the ship had not been good with a small amount of fish on board and not knowing if we would be sailing again. Being two persons short I took the deckie learner on watch with me so we had three daymen who do maintenance on the deck as well as clean the ship. Breakfast this morning had consisted of a full English with Canadian maple syrup bacon which we had ordered and it went down a treat. Relieved by the mate for lunchtime and as I turned in, the engines gathered momentum and we were now running at full speed.

We have finally reached the coast of Scotland after passing Rockall and the Flanna Islands. We are now abeam of the Butt of Lewis and this time tomorrow we shall be in the river Humber. This trip has been an experience, maybe not a lot of fish but we have seen some sights. Plenty of wild life with a few whales and dolphins. The night skies have been spectacular with shooting stars in abundance and the occasional Northern Lights giving us a display once more. The unsung hero on here, the Cook, who just gets on with things in any given weather. It's time for me to go off watch. I don't think that I will get much sleep as I'm sure that I will get the channels.

It always felt nice coming home from the fishing grounds with a decent catch of fish but it didn't happen this trip. It has been a challenge, to say the least, but what do Fishermen do? They just shrug their shoulders and get on with it. The Northern lights gave us a fine display just north of Aberdeen towards Buchaness, then the loom of the land took away our view. I came off watch at breakfast time when we were just passing Flamborough head. I then grabbed an hour of sleep on top of my bunk. When I awoke, I finished packing my gear! When the job in hand had been completed, I was then called to the bridge as it was my duty to take the ship in and out of the dock. As we were making our approaches to the Burcom (buoyage area) we received a message by the dockmaster to proceed to Hull where we were to discharge our catch. Surely nothing else can go wrong, I thought. Half of the crew were put onto the Brenda Fisher with just a skeleton crew to dock the ship.

We soon. approached Hull Fish Docks where two tugboats took us into the dock stern first. Safely moored up with a mini bus taking us to the Ferry terminal. The Skipper cleared the Bond with the Customs and off we went. We reached the Terminal with no ferry in sight. We, ended up in the MINERVA pub and had two or three pints which soon went to our heads as most people had not had a drink for a while. Soon the Ferry was in and straight to the bar for a couple more until we reached the other side. Making our way across the Humber we ran aground and an hour later we docked. We had a short walk to the train station. I looked behind me and Alf, the third engineer, was struggling to walk. As I went back to help him the train departed to Cleethorpes. I noticed a large wooden trailer and put Alf onto it. I then pulled it towards the platform. I telephoned the Wife to pick me up in the car which she duly did. My son, who had been in the back of the car looked very unsure of Alf, with his gold rimmed glasses, just muttering a few words as he was hardly able speak. I can laugh about it now but I didn't want to leave a crew mate behind. We soon dropped Alf off in Nunthorpe and then made our way Home.

The next day, which was landing day, I went down dock and met some crew members who were looking anxious. I went upstairs in Boston's Office to settle up. My turn soon approached and I knocked on the wicket to the Cashiers Department. When it opened, I was given a Settling Sheet showing that I owed the company £8.00. We had landing in debt for a 23-day trip to sea in extremely hard conditions. I was just about to walk away when I was called back to be given a tax rebate of £25. I went to see the ships runner who told us all that she won't be sailing AGAIN! We landed 900 Kit of mostly squaddies 500 and the rest being cod making £11,000 in total. With not even a fry of fish to take home!

3 days later I was asked to go in the Boston Kestrel – fishing Middle Water?????

Photographic Record

Kenny Ford and me in our youth

My Nanna in her youth

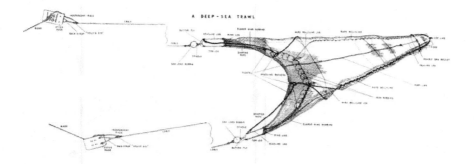

A deep sea trawl

How to rig and use a Dhan Buoy

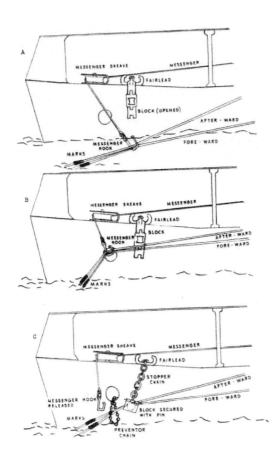

The cod line

The Otter Doors

The Winch

The Towing Block

Bobbins

Decks awash

Blowing a Hooley

Hauling in the cod end

Hauling the net

Hauling the net in

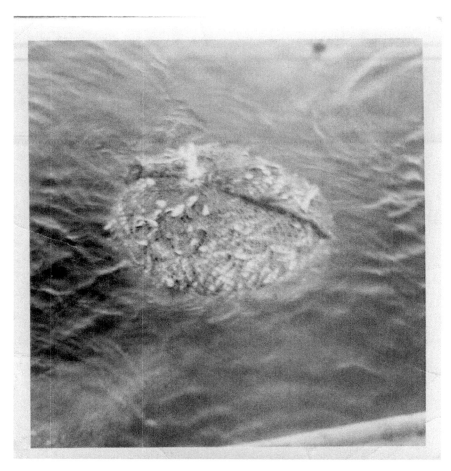

Cod ends ready to haul

Cod ends waiting to be undone

Deckie learner and sea gulls

Gutting in the fish pounds

Gutting in the fish pounds

Glossary of
Trawling Terminology

Aft The extreme end of the vessel from the bow.

Amidships The area near or at the middle of the vessel.

Backhander A sum of money given to a friend who was 'out of a ship' (i.e., not working). The man giving the backhander was known as a 'hovel'.

Backing round When trawling, this is the act of turning the ship 180 degrees round to port.

Backing off When trawling, this is the act of altering course to port.

Backstrop A wire which has three eyes, two attached to the back of the otter board, the third holds the Kelly's eye which is instrumental when attaching/detaching the otter boards.

Banana Link A shaped link that accommodates the large bow shackle which joins the two trawl door brackets, and to which the warp is attached.

Baskets A round container made from wicker in which fish catch was roughly calculated. There were approximately 3 baskets to 2 kits. A kit when measured out on the fish market was equal to 10 stone (63.5 kilo) in weight.

Becket A term used for a number of different items. The main double becket fits around the cod end and allows a large catch to be brought onboard efficiently in manageable quantities.

Bight A loop formed in a rope or wire.

Blocking up The action of containing the two warps in the towing block aft when shooting the gear.

Bobbins The heavy string of steel and rubber spheres which act as the footrope and allows the gear to stay in contact with the seabed.

Bogs The aluminium or composite floats on the headline. In Grimsby they were called 'cans'.

Bolsh A soft three strand rope attached to the leading edges of the trawl wings which is then fastened to the headline or footrope.

Bosun Short for Boatswain who was a watch keeper and in charge of the deck in the absence of the Mate.

Brackets The two triangular steel fixtures on the otter boards to which the towing warps are clipped/unclipped.

Braiding needle A small wooden instrument used to repair/braid net, when loaded with twine.

Bridge The upper part of the superstructure which contains the wheelhouse.

Bridge Telegraph The mechanical communication instrument for conveying engine movement from the wheelhouse to the engine room.

Bunk A seaman's bed.

Busters A round hotcake baked by many Cooks, usually eaten with a cup of tea between mealtimes.

Butterfly One of the components of the Dan Leno arrangement; holds the toe leg wire and the headline wire.

Cables Lengths of wire between the trawl and the trawl doors. In Grimsby they were called 'sweeps'.

Cable drum The main wire holders on the starboard and port sides of the winch for housing the warps.

Chief Engineer The head qualified Engineer in charge of and responsible for the engines and all mechanical, hydraulic and pumping equipment.

Clumpers Old cut down sea boots used as 'slippers.'

Clog Additional weight added to otter board shoe. Helps prevent the wear and tear on shoe.

Cod end The final part of a trawl net which is made of strong double twine. It contains the fish as the opening is tied off by use of the cod line.

Cod line knot A slip type of knot used specifically on the cod end. It closes off the open end but can be easily released when the catch comes onboard.

Coming round When trawling, this is the act of turning the ship 180 degrees round to starboard.

Coming to When trawling, this is the act of altering course to starboard.

Dan Lenos A part of the iron gear that is towed ahead of the main trawl attached to the ground cable. It consists of a 24-inch steel sphere through which a spindle is housed, this is connected to the butterfly section which holds the headline and toe legs.

Deckhand A proficient and usually experienced fisherman whose role is specifically deck work especially during fishing operations.

Deckie learner A young apprentice type deckhand.

Derrick A heavy duty steel arm attached to the foremast used to heave the cod ends outboard by means of a block and wire commonly referred to as a 'yo yo' wire.

Dippy giggle An odd physical condition often experienced by those who work on deck for long hours in extreme conditions. Its effect makes men laugh when generally there is little to laugh at.

Donkey The salt water hose provided to the fish washer from the engine room sea water pump. Old term for a pump engine of less than one horse power.

Door chain The heavy duty chain secured to the gallows which is used when disengaging the trawl doors during the hauling and shooting operation.

Double sheaved The heavy lift block with two rollers secured on the foremast and used with the tackle hook to bring the bag of fish inboard.

Duck Pond The lowest area on the deck where the working deck meets the raised after area and where the largest scupper is situated to allow water shipped onboard to flow out.

Fasteners Wrecks or other seabed obstructions that the trawler's gear can be caught up on and damaged or lost.

Fathom A measurement of water depth equal to 6 feet (1.83 metres).

Fireman Assistant to the Chief or Second Engineer.

Fish room The below deck section of the vessel specifically designed to hold/preserve the catch.

Fish room man A deckhand who managed the fish room.

Fleet A process whereby lengths of net are brought sequentially onboard by use of lifting gear.

Floats Aluminium or plastic spheres used to float open the headline of the trawl whilst being towed on the seabed.

Footrope The heavy-duty string of steel/rubber bobbins used to weigh the bottom of the trawl onto the seabed.

Force 4-5 Wind speed as stated on the Beaufort Scale where winds of between 13 and 24mph are experienced.

Fore Towards the bow.

Foredeck The part of the working deck between the duckpond and the whaleback.

Foul gear To have a problem with the trawl/ tangled gear.

Frap Having a problem; in a bit of chaos.

Galley The vessel's kitchen where all food is prepared and cooked.

Galley boy The Cook's assistant, the most junior rating onboard.

Gallows The horseshoe shaped large steel structures sited close to the ships rail, both aft and forward, through which the warps ran during hauling, shooting and towing of the gear.

Gash Extra sleep when watch below, due to no work until hauling time.

G Link A heavy duty G shaped link which is used to connect/disconnect the trawl warps to the otter boards.

Gilguy A wire used through a block on the wheelhouse to fleet the volume of net inboard which include the square, belly/baitings and lengtheners.

Gilson hook The hook used on the end of the Gilson wire used for most heaving tasks other than the final lift inboard of a bag of fish.

Ground cable The sweep wires located between the otter boards and the Dan Lenos.

Guiding on gear The mechanism fitted at the front of the winch which spools the warps evenly on the cable drums.

Gutting The action of removing the innards of the fish in order to prevent them spoiling.

Haddock Rash An irritable skin condition which causes a rash to the hands, wrists, forearms, when gutting haddocks which have sand, grit in the gut.

Hammerlock A modern type of shackle that comes in two parts with a locking pin.

Hauling The retrieving of the fishing gear after being towed for a given period of time.

Headline The wire reinforced top of the mouth of the trawl net which houses the spherical floats.

Helm A common term given to the process of altering the ship's rudder to change the direction of the ship's heading.

Hopper A machine used to transfer the raw livers from the deck to the liver house aft, operated by steam.

Jummy Lump A hurtful physical condition to a deckhand's wrists caused by excessive work, in the main gutting.

Keep A steel link sliced into the ground cable which, when stopped in the Kelly's eye allows the otter boards to be attached/detached.

Kelly's eye An item of ironware used within the components of a full set of gear, used specifically to capture the cable keep thereby allowing the otter boards to be connected/disconnected.

Knocking out The act of releasing the warps from the towing block.

Leeside The side opposite to the weather which gave some shelter to those working on deck.

Leggo aft A colloquial command meaning to let the warps go free from the towing block to enable hauling of the gear to take place.

Length A measurement of 25 fathoms on the trawl warps marked by intertwining rope into the wire.

Lengtheners A section of double net between the belly/baitings and the cod end. It allows space within the trawl if a large catch is made.

Liver baskets The baskets used to save the livers in during the gutting of the fish.

Liver house A section aft within which large steam operated boilers rendered the raw livers into liver oil. In some vessels the plant was situated forward.

Mate The ship's deck officer junior only to the Skipper.

Messroom The area dedicated to where the crew ate their meals and enjoyed recreation.

Officer's Mess The area onboard specifically for use by the Officers for eating/recreation.

Oilskins Waterproof clothing worn by the deckhands. Rubber, plastic suits or all-in-one frock – like garments.

Otter boards The 11 x 5 foot steel and wood constructed doors used to provide the horizontal opening to the trawl when being towed on the seabed. They were apparently named after one of the first steam trawlers to use them.

Pan of shackles A common name to describe a meat/vegetable stew.

Paying out When the warps are running outboard during the shooting of the gear.

Portside The side of a vessel that lies on your left-hand side when facing the bow (forward).

Pot of spesh Short for 'special' – a pot of tea made with the crew members' own tea rather than the Company issue.

Pound An area of the deck closed off using boards to restrict fish movement.

Preventor chain/ Restraining chain A heavy duty chain with one end secured to the gallows with the other end being free to secure the otter board during hauling/shooting of the gear.

Rigging A fixture consisting of three heavy duty wrapped wires attached to the deck at the bottom and diverging at one point on the mast below the crosstree to form a 'ladder' to climb up/down.

Scratching on Signing on the ship's Articles (a Contract) before sailing.

Scuppers Openings in the ship side plating at deck level, to allow any sea water taken onboard to run away freely. They were also a means of getting rid of guts, debris etc.

Second Engineer A qualified watchkeeping engineer junior to the Chief Engineer.

Selvedge's The edges of a net section, laced together to seal and reinforce sections of the trawl.

Sheave A roller type block through which the warps or wire can freely run through, as the ones attached at the fore and aft gallows.

Shooting The operational process of sending the fishing gear to the seabed.

Sitting Term used at mealtimes for the times the crew would eat i.e., 1200 to 1230 first sitting/1230 to 1300 second sitting.

Sittings or Settings Short lengths of twine used to secure the bolsh on the trawl wings to the headline or footrope.

Skipper The Senior Officer onboard with sole responsibility for the safety and profitability of the vessel.

Snacker A Deckie Learner.

Snottler A heavy rope used for hauling in the bellies of the net when something very heavy had been trawled up.

Splice A process whereby a rope/wire is repaired or when an eye needs to be formed.

Splodge Often used as a nickname for the younger members of the crew – Deckie Learner or Galley Boy.

Starboard The side of a vessel that lies on your right-hand side when facing the bow (forward).

Tannoid A loud hailer communication system, which links the bridge to a number of areas on the ship.

Third Hand A uncertified proficient experienced deckhand who assumes a watch keeping role usually overseen by the Skipper.

Toe leg wire A wire which forms part of the ground gear connecting the footrope to the Dan Leno.

Tow The action of trawling the fishing gear along the seabed.

Towing block Is the fix point at the stern into which the warps are safely retained while the fishing gear is being towed on the seabed. It allows the vessels to be manoeuvred by keeping the warps clear from the propeller/rudder.

TrawL The complete net part of a trawler's fishing gear.

Treacle duff A common dish, a pudding which can be produced as a savoury or with treacle as a sweet.

Twine The 'string like' material used in the production of netting.

Two blocks The term used when anything being lifted by a derrick cannot go any higher.

Wake The disturbed path of water created by the ship's propeller.

Warps Heavy duty wire that the fishing gear was towed on.

Watch A period of duty.

Whipping drums The outer barrels on a winch on which most wire/rope heaving operations take place.

Winch The main mechanical power source on deck to heavy/lift weights. It is fundamental to the hauling and shooting of the fishing gear.

Wing rubbers Rubber discs slotted onto wires which are attached to the main bobbins and form the footrope.

Wireless Operator The communications officer responsible for all transmissions on behalf of the Skipper and has total responsibility for the maintenance and repair of all electronic equipment i.e., radio, radar, echo sounders.

Available worldwide from Amazon
and all good bookstores

Michael Terence
Publishing

www.mtp.agency

www.facebook.com/mtp.agency

@mtp_agency

Printed in Great Britain
by Amazon

34742848R00152